THE
MILLIONAIRE
MIDWIFE

12 Revelations of a Profit Producer

BRANDY WOODS-SMITH

DEDICATION

This book is dedicated to…

The ones who showed me the way: My mom, Stephanie Hickombottom. My Dad, Thomas Woods. My Pops, Charles Hickombottom, and my TT Pastor, Barbara Barrett

The one who walks with me along the way: My sister, Natalie Woods-Leffall

The ones who will follow my way: My daughters and sons, Madison and McKinzey Boyd, Shawndrika, Sanya, Octavia and Shawn Smith Jr.

The one who has me all the way: My husband, Shawn Smith.

CONTENTS

FOREWORD

My Little Sister is a Big Deal

I was only three years old when my mom came home and told me she was pregnant. Call me crazy, but I distinctively remember being excited about my new baby brother. Somehow, in my three-year-old toddler brain, I assumed it would be a boy. Just two days after my fourth birthday, my mother gave birth to a tiny, adorable, bald-headed, baby GIRL! I was far from excited. How could this happen? I was supposed to be the only princess in the family and I wasn't prepared to share my throne. I remember kicking, screaming, and crying, "I want a brother. Take it back. I want a brother."

Unfortunately, life doesn't offer a refund or exchange policy on siblings. I was forced to welcome my baby sister, Brandy Nicole Woods into my life. She often tells stories of how I tortured her when we were growing up. I have zero recollection of those violations (that's my story and I'm sticking to it). I honestly don't remember abusing Brandy, but I do recall simply tolerating her existence. Like many little sisters, Brandy was a nuisance. She was bothersome … annoying … inconvenient. But one day something shifted. I was in my senior year at Sam Houston State University and Brandy was preparing for her freshman year at Jarvis Christian college on a full academic scholarship (she may have been irritating, but she was always intelligent). On the eve of this new chapter of my sister's life, I felt an enormous burden to protect her from the world and all its trickery. I moved from tolerating the bratty little girl who should've been a boy, to celebrating the smart young woman who was destined for greatness.

Brandy didn't have to follow in my footsteps, she paved her own way. She mastered education by earning Teacher of the Year and then moved on to be the first and the youngest African-American Math Coordinator in a predominately white school district. She slew business by taking a leap of faith and opening *Imagine Me Academy* and turning it into the premiere early childhood education center in the community in which she was raised. And now, Brandy dominates the world by not only being the midwife to those who desire to earn millions, but by being a walking example of how $12, unspeakable faith, hard work, determination, and a big sister who loves you unconditionally can catapult you into unimaginable wealth and prosperity. As you read this book, I pray you are inspired to tap into the millionaire that lives within. I'm so glad I didn't get that baby brother I thought I so desperately wanted. Brandy has proved herself to be a great little sister, and she is a much bigger deal than I could ever imagine.

ACKNOWLEDGEMENTS

There are so many emotions I feel right now. I feel proud that I FINALLY accomplished a lifelong goal of being a published author. Being excited about what is to come would describe me perfectly. The feeling that stands out the most is gratitude.

I would like to thank all of my fellow Powerhouses, friends and collaborators. In the last few years, I have been surrounded with so much love and support. Together we have grown, cried and overcome so many obstacles. We made it.

A special thanks to Rochelle Chapman and Marilyn J. Lewis for helping me in the final hours of this project. Sharon Jenkins you are a superstar and a master literary coach. Without you this book would still be in my belly. You continued to help me PUSH until I birthed this baby, just as a midwife should. Your expertise, judgement and encouragement was priceless.

My family is the best. The bond we have is unbreakable. I have a host of cousins, uncles and aunties that have supported me without fail. Thank you. A special thanks to my TT Pastor,

Barbara Barrett! Thanks for all the prayers, encouraging words and wise counsel.

Mom and Pop (Charles and Stephanie Hickombottom) thanks for every night you babysat, all the support and belief in my dreams and never doubting they would come true.

My sister, Natalie Woods-Leffall, is my EVERYTHING. But, you all already know that. Nat, thanks for clearing the path for greatness. When I see you, I see a superhero. SUPER SISSY!

Motherhood has been one of my greatest accomplishments. I was blessed to birth two wonderful daughters, McKinzey and Madison. But make no mistake, I am a mother of six. In 2012, I was blessed with four beautiful children Shawndrika, Octavia, Shawn and Sanya. We were blessed with Leah Sky, our first grand-baby. I love you all so much and see so much potential in you. My sincere desire is that you will be true to your dreams and aspirations. There are no limits to what you can do. Keep God first. I am proud of you all. You all are my favorite!

Hey Bae! What a man.... a mighty good man. Yes, he is! Thank you for being my rock. Thank you for being everything I needed. There is no doubt that the life we are creating will exceed our wildest expectations.

And last but not least, I want to thank myself, Mrs. Brandy Woods-Smith. Hey Girl! We have been through a lot, but we made it. For every tear, expect joy. Thanks for getting back up every time we got knocked down. Thanks for putting your big girl panties on when times got tough and PUSHING forward. Thank you for loving me and forgiving me when I made mistakes. Most of all thanks for standing on the word of GOD concerning our life! Don't stop now, we have an army of millionaires to create. Much gratitude to *The Millionaire Midwife*.

INTRODUCTION

Millionaire - a person whose a sets are worth one million dollars or more.

If you are a person who desires to possess "assets worth one million dollars or more," you are in the right place at the right time. Reading The Millionaire Midwife will put you in a strategic position to make a decision to change the course of wealth in your life.

You are more than a window shopper... you are actually serious about living a prosperous life. You've voluntarily crossed the bridge of "I can't" into "I can" be a millionaire and you are looking for a way to achieve that esteemed status of wealth. Look no further, you have found it! I wrote this book to drive home the fact it doesn't matter where you start in life, but how you finish is extremely important.

The Millionaire Midwife helps you establish a millionaire mindset which will assist you in building a business or career that will propel you into your purpose. Get ready to hear cha-ching, cha-ching in your bank account as you implement the success revelations that have empowered me to live a life I once thought was impossible. With God, all things are possible and because of His faithfulness and wisdom, I can now live a life others are still dreaming about. Don't get stuck with your head on the pillow of complacency. Read on and be empowered to produce wealth!

REVELATION 1

Sometimes Rock Bottom is the Best Place to Start

Let us not become weary in doing good,

for at the proper time we will reap

a harvest if we do not give up.

Galatians 6:9 KJV

How It All Began

At the age of 17, I experienced devastation like no other. My father passed away. Just one week before I was due to leave for college. His death propelled me on a path that was unexpected and challenging. Mourning his death and leaving home the same week was the hardest thing I have ever experienced. But I wanted to honor him by getting my education. You see, his father died the Summer before he was to start college as well. Not going to college was one of his regrets. I always knew I wanted to attend college. I dreamed of pursuing a business or marketing degree at NYU, but since my father was no longer here, I did not want my mother to bear the responsibility of paying for my education so I COMPROMISED.

Thanks to a recommendation from Colleen Walker, my high school teacher, from the College of Education, I received a full ride scholarship to Jarvis Christian College and graciously took it. Although this was not my career plan, I made the best of it. I obtained my Bachelor's of Science in Mathematics and my teacher's certification. I became a great teacher and ultimately honed my craft as an educator. I still use the skills I gained at that time today. When I fell in love with teaching, I feel hard. Jarvis Christian College was amazing. I can still remember how clear the night sky was, the dorm wars, and having to drive miles just to get to a grocery store. I had a really great time there. I met lifelong friends and the laughs were endless. I pledged my beloved sorority, Alpha Kappa Alpha Sorority, Incorporated. It was the best of times.

My sophomore year, I ended up meeting my college sweetheart. I was young and in love so we decided to get married when I was 20 years of age one month after I graduated. Although he was sweet, our marriage wasn't. Our relationship was the poster child for unhealthy love. Even though things were rocky, I believed we could work it out. I didn't come from a family where divorce was common. My grandparents had been married for 50 years. My mother has been married to my stepfather for 32 years. Divorce was not my ideal solution in my eyes.

Things rapidly changed for the worst. The final straw came in 2007. I was at the hospital awaiting my new bundle of joy to come into this world and share it with my husband when he brought his 19-year-old girlfriend to the hospital. My heart sank and I knew at this moment I had hit rock bottom. My marriage had failed. I made a decision that day I would no longer turn back to that unhealthy relationship. So I got divorced.

I remember the day so vividly. The months had been heartbreaking. I hadn't seen him in months. I was prepared. I presented him the divorce papers right there in the hospital. It was a bittersweet day. A day that changed the course of my life forever. Once discharged, I went back home to live with my parents. I had left all the furniture, clothes, dishes, and household goods. I came home with a Master's degree and $12 to my name. I literally started over with my daughter's diaper bag and my purse.

We all have a turning point in our life, a moment in time where we see things clearly, the good, bad, and the ugly. This was one of those moments.

Even in the midst of my heartache God gave me my daughters as a parting gift. Madison was my salvation. I know if I was not carrying life, I probably would've given up. I was never suicidal, but I did have some homicidal moments. I know, I wouldn't have bounced back as quickly.

McKinzey was my inspiration; I probably wouldn't have bounced back so quickly without the responsibility of mothering her. She helped me develop unconditional love, patience and longsuffering which fueled my staying power. So with both of my children God taught me different lessons.

Just when I thought things were getting better, on the eve of my 30th birthday I was notified by my doctor there was a possibility I may have cancer. I was paralyzed with fear. I went to my doctor and they informed me that I had tumors. They began the PET scans which validated their existence. The plan was surgery. They scheduled it within a few weeks of my diagnosis.

The day of my surgery was one of the scariest days of my life. I can remember my mom telling me that everything would be alright even though her eyes said something different. My IV was started; I was prepped and wheeled into the operating room. They cut me open only to find the Great Physician had already removed every trace of a tumor. There was no evidence in my body of any tumors! Thank God living with cancer never became my reality, but this health scare came at one of the worst times in my life. Once again I found out how resilient I was. I was ready to go after my passion. I turned my focus to creating the life I'd always dreamed of, it was my time to take control.

Decided to Make a Change

I went back to teach in the public-school system and fast tracked in my career. I became an administrator and began to develop my leadership skills. A few years later, I received a position as a curriculum director. (I had become indispensable). Right? I hired a great friend to take my position because I was granted a promotion as Director of Schools. I trained her for my job in May and June then went on vacation. When I walked back into the office everything had changed. "Even the air seemed thicker."

The position I was promoted to became extinct when my supervisor had an untimely change of heart. I had already signed the contract and assumed the position. I had finally gotten to a place where I had a stable job with more money than I had ever made. I was living on my own only to receive another setback in my career. I had to fight for my severance package. I had to go to war for unemployment. Even in the midst of turmoil, God was still pushing me closer to my dream.

"My lifetime goal was to open my own school". Once education crept into my heart, I was in love. I dreamed and imagined what the classrooms would look like, the building, children, etc. For seven years I pondered this. When circumstances prevailed, it was time to make my dream a reality. From the day I left my prior position, it took me only seven weeks to open my school. God was walking with me the entire time.

The year before I went from a public school to a charter school. I had never worked in a charter school before, but I made more money that year than I had made in the last two years combined. I ended up clearing a little over $100,000 for the first time and that didn't even include my side hustles! This gave me the rest of the money to do everything I needed to do. Everyone pitched in. My sister gave me the last five thousand dollars to open my business. My mom and my dad gave me an old dilapidated building to start my school. It was approximately 1,500 square feet and I could only take 20 kids. I was definitely in the wilderness, but God healed me there. I didn't have to answer to anyone but Him.

My dreams were finally coming true. I was definitely in the wilderness, but God healed me there. I didn't have to answer to anyone but Him.

The building was in desperate need of repair and a miracle. God sent me two angels in the form of my cousin, Darryl Brooks and my boyfriend Shawn Smith. They were my miracle renovators and as a result, my school passed all the necessary inspections with flying colors. Little did I know that Shawn would help renovate my life. Seven years later, we married and I became Brandy Woods-Smith.

During my first week I opened with two kids and only made $800 the first month. My mom and I worked 60-hour weeks with only two kids enrolled, but over the course of the year we were able to move into an 8,000-square foot building. We had outgrown the capacity of the school in less than one year. We went from making $800 a month to making about $25,000 a month in revenue in less than two years. Today our growth still amazes me as we continue to shatter my expectations. With multiple locations, we project 100K months are just around the corner.

Being faithful to the business and to the vision God had given me was the key to our success. I started using the principles in the Bible, speaking powerful affirmations over my business. For example, "He really had given me the ability to get wealth" and "He has already anointed my purpose for kingdom success." Even though I didn't see it by faith, it had already been done.

I really am anchored in the passage of scripture in Hebrews 11, where in the Bible the Apostle Paul recounts "by faith" how Abraham did it, "by faith" how Moses did it, "by faith" how Rahab did it, etc. I began to use that passage as a staple for declaring things over my business that by faith I'm also going to accomplish what God has for me to accomplish.

The flip side is "faith without works is dead," (James 2:26) so I established a very strong work ethic. I began to work as "unto the Lord." Even in the way that I treated my employees was as "unto the Lord." I was determined to honor God with my stewardship and service in building the school. It took me hitting rock bottom in order to go full force after my dream and at that point I knew I could only work for me and Jesus.

Assuming a Position of Faith

Trust in the Lord with all your heart, And lean not on your own understanding; In all your ways acknowledge Him, And He shall [a]direct your paths.   Proverbs 3: 5-6 (NKJV) A position of faith is vital to success. When all else fails, you have to see beyond what you see in the natural. I now have a lot of opportunities where I work in collaboration with other people, but I first had to allow God to build me as an entrepreneur and my business for growth and success. I think every Christian entrepreneur has to get to the point where Jesus is your business partner, but you have to do your part. You must have faith God will give you the ideas and the anointing, but you have to roll up your sleeves do the work.

When the Israelites needed to get beyond the wall of Jericho, God gave them the idea to walk around the wall. He also gave them the revelation to shout on the seventh time around to cause it to come crumbling down. God gave them the strategy, but they had to do the work. If you think about Noah, God told Noah to build an ark. He gave him the strategy to the smallest detail. But if Noah hadn't done the work, then Noah wouldn't have reaped the fruits of his labor. If Abraham had not left his family and his comfortable situation, he would not have become the father of many nations.

The rock bottom place is where you know it's you and God and He's telling you what to do. Then by faith, you put it in action. Your tools are prayer, His Word and faith. God gives you the anointing for the job. Rock bottom is the best place to start because you're throwing out everything you thought you could depend on and moving forward by faith. Sometimes the relationships you thought you could depend on are not there anymore. The resources you thought you could count on are all gone. In this place you learn the good, the bad, and the ugly about yourself, but you also learn that "I Am that I Am" is with you. God has to become more to you than just the Lord of your life. He has to become your peace, protection, your way, and He has to walk with you through the battlefield to your victory. God truly becomes Emmanuel, God with us.

"There are things that you learn in the valley, that you will never learn on the mountaintop." I believe in the rock-bottom wilderness moments; you really get to see God as more than the Lord of your life. When it comes to entrepreneurship or reshaping your life those rock bottom moments are the building blocks where you can lay a solid foundation. During this process, you discover the fragile things that are not stable, will crumble and fall by the wayside.

I remember reading Psalm 91 and asking God during this time to hide me under the shadow of His wings until I was strong enough to walk. I asked Him to be my everything: an enemy to my enemies, my protector, confidant, and my friend. Even though a lot of times in this season I was alone, I wasn't lonely. I got reacquainted with myself and prioritized what was important to me and for my children. I also discovered my God given purpose and who He needed me to be. This is one of the reasons I can speak to people when they feel like they have no hope. If I can go through losing my dad, a failed marriage, losing my job, and having a cancer scare, you can go through it too and win.

Literally, I feel like God gave me a second chance and all of this happened in the same season. I was so overwhelmed until I came to the place where it was just me and God. Of course, he gave me my family, friends, a support system, but at the end of the day, it was just me and Him. He was enough for me and He is enough for you. Rock bottom is the place of new beginnings when God is in charge of your life.

"Against all hope, Abraham in hope believed and so became the father of many nations, just as it had been said to him! "So shall your offspring be." Without weakening in his faith, he faced the fact that his body was as good as dead—since he was about a hundred years old—and that Sarah's womb was also dead. Yet he did not waver through unbelief regarding the promise of God, but was strengthened in his faith and gave glory to God, being fully persuaded that God had power to do what he had promised (See Romans 4:18 - 21).

Are you fully persuaded? I am!

REVELATION 2

Fear is Not Your Enemy

Have I not commanded thee?
Be strong and of a good courage; be not afraid,
neither be thou dismayed: for the Lord thy
God is with thee whithersoever thou goest.
Joshua 1:9, KJV

Fear is not your enemy! The purpose of this Revelation is to investigate how fear is a natural response system that we can use for our advantage in building wealth. It is a God-given mechanism which allows you to use your instinct to know when you should or should not do something or when you're in danger. It also acts as a spiritual GPS that warns you when something isn't quite right. According to Joyce Meyer, "Everyone experiences fear in their life. There are big fears we are very aware of and little ones we may not even realize we have. I've learned that it's very important to understand what fear is and how it works against us because if we don't, it can keep us from becoming what God created us to be, which means we won't fulfill our purpose in life."

To get where you want to go in life, you have to face fear. You can make fear an enemy or allow it to act as a divine compass, illuminating your steps to a greater destiny. God encourages His people to "fear not" 365 times in the bible. His overall message is simply do not be afraid, instead, be full of faith. Because "without faith it is impossible to please God." (Hebrew 11:6, NIV)

Fear is both an internal and external response. Sometimes the fear that you feel makes you actually go back and check on something you should have done. Whenever there is a hesitation to do something, I call that baby fear. Then there is giant fear, the fear that literally stops you from doing something because you have a fear of failing. Some people are even afraid of succeeding. Then there is a fear of leaving people out or the fear of not fitting in. There are too many types of fear to name here, but you get the message.

I talk to people all the time that are paralyzed by fear. They may say, "I went to school for this, so I am a supposed to do this?" Who told you, you were supposed to do that? We take on the plans of other people and make them our own. We box ourselves in and silence our greatness. We don't live up to our fullest potential because of fear.

Self-talk

Self-talk often influences how we respond to situations and circumstances. There is positive self-talk, and negative self-talk. Negative self-talk will destroy you. Some examples are: "You're going to look foolish." "Who's going to pay you for this?" "You don't have what it takes?"

Positive self-talk says things like, "Let's investigate what else we can do." "Let's do what makes us happy." It is often easier for us to embrace the negative self-talk than the positive self-talk. So, we talk ourselves out of doing some things we want to because we have the fear of it not working out.

A lot of times, we don't do things because when we see the calculated cost, it's more than we're willing to give up. The fear of spending a lot of time and money and it not working out scares us. We're just not willing to take the risk. Then sometimes, we wrestle with the negative self-talk that tells us we're not adequate, don't know enough, we don't know enough people, that we're not likable enough, we don't have the right appearance nor have the right tools. These things are the destroyer of dreams.

One of the ways that you combat negative self-talk is you must face it head on. Ask yourself what's the worst that can happen in this scenario? "Could I lose my home? What if I lose all my savings?" If we look at the "what's the worst that could happen" scenario, we can deflate fear.

Self-talk usually stems from something from our past or someone else's opinion. We have to find the root of the self-talk because maybe we've let a tragic event from our past or someone else's opinion become our own. For example, will let the teacher tell you you're not good in Math, so for the rest of your life you say you're not good in Math. Or someone tells you that you are messy and for the rest of your life you feel like you should be disorganized. Honestly, these things are skills which can be acquired, they're not innate. Everything is a learned behavior and even if something is a character flaw, the Bible says in 1 John 3:20, "If our hearts condemn us, we know that God is greater than our hearts, and he knows everything." God is bigger than our heart and our flaws.

If there's something in your character you need to change then go to your God, your heavenly Father and say, "OK God, help me work out these character issues, so I don't have to walk in fear." If you know you're dishonest, that's going to hurt your business and it is a character trait that you need to work on. If you know you don't have good follow through, or you don't keep your word, then that's something that you're going to have to work on. Over time, you can do the right thing long enough to overcome that flaw.

Affirmations

Self-talk is a task that we all must master, whether it is negative or positive, we all have it. How do we increase our positive self-talk? We do that by making positive affirmations. We can use Biblical affirmations, or it could be a simple affirmation that says, "I can do this." Just as simple as that, and you tell yourself every day, "I can do this." After you tell yourself something so many times, your subconscious mind will say, "we can do this." You will begin to see yourself doing it. It's just like eating right and exercising. Practicing something increases the probability that it will become a permanent habit. The more you tell yourself you can do it, the more confidence you have.

Faith comes by hearing, hearing by the word. It could be the word of God, but it could also be the words you're telling yourself, time and time again. So, having a good set of affirmations is invaluable to successfully building wealth. I also suggest that everybody writes a written affirmation about themselves. You know who you are. You are a child of the King. You are capable and able to accomplish everything that you want to accomplish. You're loving, caring, kind, and you have enough compassion to reach nations. Begin to tell yourself that you are equipped by God with everything that you need and all the tools that you need are readily at your disposal. Decree that everything that you want or need is either in your hand or on its way to you, you are the attraction to all of the wealth and resources that you need in your life.

If you begin to tell yourself these things every day, through self-manifestation and self-prophecy, you will find these things coming to you. That's why it's important to read the Word of God because it begins to be ingrained in you and you begin to tell yourself that you're the head and not the tail, that you're the lender and not the borrower, that you are above and not beneath, that you have the solution that others are looking for, that you have the power to create, that you have the power to get well, that God is doing a new thing in you, that old things are passed away and all things are becoming new in your life.

As you begin to create an affirmation statement for your life, and begin to read these things, they will become deeply rooted in who you are. When things get tough, it's going to bubble up and it's going to defeat the negative self-talk. For example, when your body says, "I'm tired, how am I going to overcome this?" You will begin to hear that in God, you're more than a conqueror, that with God, nothing is impossible, that your present from God is the mark of the high calling, that you're not double minded but you are single minded so that you're stable, that God has not given you the spirit of fear, He's given you love, power and a sound mind. The more you begin to say that affirmation to yourself and do positive self-talk, the more the negative self-talk goes away, it loses its power.

Negative self-talk is always going to be there, but now you have something to fight it with. If you were a fireman, if you saw a fire, you would get the hose and would combat the fire. It's not that the fire is not going to come. If there was no fire, we wouldn't need firemen. It's not that the negative talk is not going to come, but over time you will build up a resistance with positive affirmations and by incorporating the Word of God. This gives you a supernatural power because we know the Word of God cannot return unto us void but it will definitely accomplish what it's sent out to do. (see Isaiah 55:11)

Journaling

Journaling is a great way to overcome fear. A lot of times, we have to clear up our mental space in order to separate fact from fiction. Our minds often create scenarios that are not true, like people don't like us; I'm not good enough for the opportunity; my family will not support me. Sometimes it's really self-created. But when you journal, especially if you can journal without censoring yourself, you can really get to what's on your mind and in your heart.

Journaling can be another form of prayer. There is a point in journaling, just like in prayer, where you break through and you don't even know what you're writing anymore. In your prayer time, you'll start out praying in yourself, but over time, the Holy

Ghost will take over that prayer. The same thing happens in journaling. You start out with selfish motives and you break through to a self-conscious journaling where you're genuinely writing about what's inside of you. You begin to the journal without censoring yourself.

Some days when I journal, I feel a boldness flowing forth on the paper. Then there are days where my journaling is light and bubbly. When you journal, even your handwriting is a symbol of how you feel that day. Journaling also allows you to go back and see your growth and what you've overcome. One of the things that we fear is that we might stop before we actually achieve our goals. But when you journal, you will see how you are getting better and better. You will examine your confidence daily, investigating those hidden fears, and also recognize the accomplishments you've overlooked.

One of the first journals that I complete at the beginning of every month is one that chronicles everything that I've accomplished the month before. It helps me go into the month, knowing that I've completed something. I can start the month on a positive footing allowing me freedom to complete everything I need to do with a sense of accomplishment.

I challenge you to start your month or your day saying, "What are the things I've accomplished?" This puts positivity in the forefront. Don't think about what you can't do, think about what you've already done and then build on those strengths to get done what you need to get done.

A common phrase that describes fear is "false evidence appearing real." You hear that all the time. Don't let the false evidence keep you from making a choice to accomplish your goals despite your reservations. Face it anyway! Going after what you want. You may be asking yourself the following, "Knowing everything that I know, how can I push back past these feelings of inadequacy, anxiety, or uncertainty and move towards my goal?" Fear is a mechanism you can use to let you know what you need to do in certain situations. So, if you feel inadequate, investigate what will make you feel adequate. Sometimes fear is just a barometer to lead you to the truth. For example, if I feel disorganized and frustrated, I'm not going to be able to successfully execute my plan for wealth. Instead of operating in fear, ask yourself, "What would I need to do to be an overcomer in this situation?" Use the fear thermostat to push past anxiety and uncertainty and find solutions.

Reach out for help. There's nothing wrong with reaching out for help to overcome your fear. It may be that you need to reach out to an expert, coach, Pastor, or to a friend and talk through the situation. They can help you identify what's real in your situation or what is not real or valid.

Fear will always show up in some way or another at different levels of your journey. Be prepared to use fear as a thermostat to decide what you need to do. Then, use your positive self-talk to overcome the fear. It's not a bad thing, it's just helping you identify the things that you need to address. Remember fear not… because God is with you!

"And the LORD said unto Moses, Behold, thou shalt sleep with thy fathers; and this people will rise up, and go a whoring after the gods of the strangers of the land, whither they go to be among them and will forsake me, and break my covenant which I have made with them." Deuteronomy 31:16, KJV.

REVELATION 3

A Winner's DNA

"For I know the plans I have for you,"
declares the Lord "plans to prosper you and not to
harm you, plans to give you hope and a future."
Jeremiah 29:11, NIV

Determination, clarity, and persistency are the key elements of a winner's personality. This dynamic combination allows the person to go from the conception of an idea to actually bringing the idea into manifestation. I use the word DNA because some of these qualities are ingrained in you. We have a natural tendency to win. Some people are just born with leadership qualities. They're able to take calculated risks, lead with precision, and they have a lot of natural talents and skills. But, don't count out the person who you think is quiet and uninterested. Many times, quiet people are very persistent and have a keen clarity when it comes to problem solving. It's not always the one with the greatest visible ability who will be the winner. Persistency, determination and your clarity help you stick with it when things get difficult. In order to win, you must have all three of these things working in your favor, but the power comes when they work at the same time.

Having a teachable spirit is vitally important when you want to win. If we're willing to identify and learn the things we don't know, then winning may be in your future. Part of being a winner is knowing straight off the bat that you don't have all the answers. Think about a relationship between the coach and the player. The player wears the crown, but without the correct coaching, without ample strength building, without the correct strategy, they would never be put in a position to win. Playing the game or opening a business is one thing. Identifying exactly what you need to know and to do is another thing. Being able to learn the skills, stamina and the strategy to actually win often comes from an external force. A lot of times it's not your internal DNA that gets you there. Every winner needs a mentor, coach or midwife. The right force behind you will ensure your success.

You will need to be taught some key elements to be a winner. We can learn through education, experience, or vicariously through other people, mistakes or successes.

None of us wants to fail in business. There are different types of people who start businesses. I've broken them down into three distinct personalities; The Idealist, The Realist, and The Strategist.

The Idealist

Initially first-time business owners are so excited. They are overjoyed with the possibility of what could happen. However, the more they get into it and really see what it takes to build a successful business, they may change their minds. That initial business honeymoon comes to an end and the longer they stay in business, the faster reality becomes less attractive. They realize that this may be a little harder than it seems and a lot of times some people stop right there. They come to the point where they decide that they don't want to put in the hard work it takes to win.

The Realist

Now some people push a little further than that and they do the work and they start experiencing some success. I call this person, The Realist. They don't have a false sense of hope; they understand what it takes to make their business work. They make the decision that they're willing to put in the work.

The Strategist

The third group of people are The Strategists. The Strategists are a group of people who really see their business as a success and they're excited and stimulated to the point that the amount of hard work doesn't matter. They put in the work and they see exactly what it takes and they're able to develop systems to make the work easier. They strategize and are able to calculate the work and the reward. They don't quit in the process because they have long-term strategies that predict.

At every juncture in your business or even in your life, you're going to have to make the decision to keep going, quit or go another way to achieve success. Honestly, every business won't succeed. Every investment won't pay-off. However, the more you utilize your skills, learn your industry and build your business muscle, you will be able to analyze a business for viability. As you become a Strategist, you will be able to take your business from concept to reality.

In business you have to make the decision not to quit, even when it gets hard. The only time that it's okay to quit is when you have identified that there is no possibility for this business to succeed. Then you do want to abort the mission and go with a more feasible option. But you can't quit just because it gets hard. In every business there is going to be a point where it gets difficult and it seems like it's not working. 1. Ask yourself, 'Is it because you're not working hard enough?' 2. Do you need to make an adjustment? 3. Is the idea flawed? The idea will let you know rather to pursue or abort.

The Heart of a Champion

A champion is not a person who has won one battle, a champion has won numerous battles and oftentimes have defied the odds to win them. A champion is a person who has time after time been victorious. Think about a boxer. A boxer can have a lot of different methods for winning rounds and a boxing match. They may lose a round but still win the match. No one becomes a champion or failure after one round. A champion has so many winnings that undeniably you have to see them as a champion. It doesn't mean they've won every round. Over time, they have consistently won and they have been a champion. They've been through the thick of the battle, with the bruises, the cuts, being knocked down, but they still prevailed. They've won enough battles to qualify for the title. Being a champion is not about winning the battle, it's about winning the war.

The heart of a champion at first starts with the individual having a will to do something. Nobody's going to stick with a goal or stay in the fight if they don't have a strong will to win. They must possess a strong yearning that's bigger than their pain and disappointment to keep going. It's bigger than a moment of failure or a moment of success because a champion knows that one moment of success is not the end of a game. Your will have to be strong enough to hold the conviction of what you're doing is right, because there's going to be many people telling you to stop when things get rough. They'll say things like, "You don't have to go through this." "There's an easier way," or "Why don't you just get a job." But you have to keep pushing.

If you really believe in your cause, business, or in your ministry, the will to see it through is rooted inside of you. A perfect will can propel you to keep working even when it gets hard. You must be able to see that your cause, visions and ministry is bigger than you. The heart of a champion is knowing that you're not even the focal point of what you're doing. There is a bigger expected outcome or result that connects you to your purpose, pain, failure and success.

There is a group of people that only you can reach. If you don't do it, then they won't be reached. Sometimes winning means not putting yourself first for a moment so that the cause can live on. It almost requires you to be a martyr for your business or for your ministry. You distinctly know that in the end, if you do right by people and your business and if you help enough people get what they want, you'll ultimately get what you want.

The heart of a champion is rooted in God. From a Christian entrepreneurial perspective, we know that with God everything is possible. Even though things are going to happen, we realize all things work together for the good, to them that love God, and are called according to his purpose. (see Romans 8:28)

The heart of a champion is a heart built in resilience. God gives us hind feet that enable us to walk victoriously over every crack and crevice on the mountains of life. Even when we don't see our victory, whether if we are in a feast or famine season, or when we're facing or impossible task, we're willing to stick with the mission to the end. You win. Whether it's in your business or ministry, a family crisis, if you are willing to get through the tough part, you win. Most people just won't keep going, it's easier to give up.

Talk is cheap. It's easier to say I'm going to change my habits than actually do it. It's easier to stop than to keep going. It's easier to stay in your current situation than to change. (It doesn't mean you're not going to be happy, it just means you're not going to live in the fullness of what God called you to live into).

It's so much easier to take the low road but when you make a decision to take the road less traveled, you have to know that all parts of that road are not going to be paved; there's going to be some trees and obstacles you're going to have to tear down. There will not be as many people on that road, so you're going to have to depend on your relationship with God and yourself to keep you through some low moments.

There will be many people who will not understand your journey. Connecting to a coach or a mentor is key on this journey. You will need someone in your life that can help you. Having a mentor who has traveled the same way may be the key factor to your resilience and success.

Think back to the story of Gideon, God called him a man of Valor. He really didn't see it in himself. He's thinking, "God, I'm hiding behind in a cave". I am not here to fight. Sometimes you have to make a decision to be a champion when God says so. God saw something in him that wasn't visible to most. Don't mistake the fact that because you're not acting as a champion, that the heart of the champion is not in you. God made you. He clearly sees the heart of a man. So, He knew Gideon was a man of valor before it ever manifested. God is calling Gideon out and Gideon is attempting to abandon God's call. Miraculously he decided to be obedient. In doing so, he finds out for himself he was indeed a champion. It's okay if you're not the champion Gideon right now. You can still be the champion God designed you to be. You can have a Gideon revelation.

Protect Your Vision

I am a firm believer what we share with the wrong people at the wrong time when it comes to our vision and our dream can abort them. A person without vision will never understand your vision. If that person doesn't have a vision for their own life, they will never be able to grasp yours. Your vision will always be bigger than your ability. It wouldn't be a vision if you could get it today. It's always going to be something that you're working towards. The first way we protect our vision is to be careful who we give our vision to. Are you putting your vision in the hands of robbers who are going to steal it? Are you putting your vision in the hands of murderers who are going to kill it? You must think about who are you placing your pearls before? Who are you sharing this vision with?

Joseph was another great champion. If Joseph hadn't told his brothers about the dream, they probably wouldn't have sold him into slavery. We sometimes have the tendency to put our dreams in the hands of robbers and murderers. People who put so much negativity and fear and doubts in us. We sometimes end up miscarrying or avoiding our dream altogether.

The second way we protect our vision is making sure that we are continually working towards the vision. Do not let a season of drought come where you're not watering and nurturing your. You can have a great idea and it can fail just because you didn't nurture it. There is a time for that ideal impact. There's a point in time for what you're supposed to be doing and sometimes that time can pass. You can pass up on an opportunity that can cost you dearly. People passed up an opportunity of your nature. How many people passed up Apple, Microsoft and investing in Facebook in the beginning? Those same individuals now look back on those days and say, "Man I missed a out." Timing is essential. Be aware of timing for your vision. What is needed to foster that vision?

The third thing is covering your vision in prayer and in the Word of God from a spiritual aspect. Covering your business in prayer and then the word, making sure that you're keeping God as a part of your business and decisions. Make sure that you are tuned into Him and what He's saying about your business.

David had a heart of a champion, he went out knowing God was with him time after time. These experiences filled him up to the brim. It wasn't because of his ability or his size. In fact, all of his brothers were bigger and stronger than him, but he had the heart and God. God looks at the heart of the man. David loved God. Even when David disappointed God, he was crying and asking for forgiveness. In his travails, he always knew his victory was connected to God. He never underestimated the fact that his ability to win had to do with the anointing put on him by the Prophet Samuel who came from God. He stayed connected to God. It was not the battle, women, mission, or his intelligence that made him victorious. His relationship with God was his staying power.

We are already a part of the body of Christ; the battle is already won. It's just about walking in the manifestation. You've already won. You just have to put in the work to get your victory crown.

REVELATION 4

Time Waits on No Man

"I must work the works of him that sent me,
while it is day: the night cometh,
when no man can work."
John 9:4, KJV

Time is a valuable variable that should not be wasted. Knowing what you want to do and when you want to do it is imperative to obtaining your millionaire status. It is human nature to procrastinate, especially when something not in your zone of genius, tedious or difficult. However, opportunity often comes at the most inconvenient time and if you aren't ready to take advantage of it, it may just slip away from you and never return. When you postpone building your network, or investing the sweat equity into your business that it required for it to be successful, you delay your progress.

Having a clear set of goals and writing the vision and making it plain, are key components to fighting procrastination. Once you know what you want to do the next step is to. Your plan is a roadmap that will get you to your destination. We will talk more about how to do that in Revelation 6. But, now let's discuss the #1 enemy to you accomplishing your goals: distractions.

Distractions

Distractions are anything that pulls you away from fulfilling your daily, monthly, yearly or lifetime goals. They can be diversions, interruptions, disturbances, interferences, or hindrances that send you into mental distress or hysteria. Things like: there's an accident on the road to work that makes you late for work; a 2:00 am telephone call that a relative has passed; a workman mowing the lawn outside of your window when you are writing a book; someone steals your parking space at the grocery store; or you developing a cold before a major presentation. These are all distractions that could ruin anyone's day and put you in a foul mood, anger, sadness or even paralysis. Anything which appeals to the five senses can be a distraction. For example, a handsome or beautiful member of the opposite sex (sight); someone who has on your favorite aftershave (smell); listening to your favorite musical artist (hearing); chocolate covered strawberries (taste); and the loving sensation when you are hugged properly (touch).

Distractions have the power to pull you off course. They can be deadly if you don't know how to recognize them. I suggest that you do the following in order to stay focused on your plan to achieve millionaire status:

1. Review your plan on a regular basis to be reminded of your immediate and short-term goals

2. Be intentional about staying on track.

3. Learn to identify distractions and develop a strategy to eliminate them as soon as possible.

4. Schedule time for those distractors that are necessary. For example: Cell phones, social media posting and review, and family time.

5. Take it one thing at a time. Remember multi-tasking may be something that you can do, but it doesn't give you the maximum result.

6. Take a scheduled break. Release, refresh, and relax daily, because self care is just as important to your success as anything else.

7. Get an accountability partner to help you stay focused if you need some help.

8. Be the captain. Remember, you have a goal to accomplish and sometimes life will get in the way, but it's up to you to put things back in order. You can do it!

Procrastination - the action of delaying or postponing something.

We can be our own worst enemies, especially when we procrastinate. For some, it's more of a problem than others. The root of the problem is often fear. Fear I will not be good enough. Fear of the unknown. Rear of failure and the fear of success. They all contribute to procrastination.

There is a simple remedy for procrastination: perseverance. Pushing past fear and staying the course until you reach your destination or fulfilling your objective will eliminate a tendency to procrastinate. PUSH until you are again moving in the right direction. Persevering is a state of mind that you have to adopt as a remedy anytime fear stares you in the face. Regardless of its root, fear can be defeated when you decide that you are going to accomplish everything that you've decided to do. The luxury of procrastination costs you too much. It may even cost you your dream. Remember to PUSH when you're shaking in your boots. What's on the other side is worth the extra effort to stay focused.

Calendar and Time Blocking

When you plan your time, you plan your success. If you don't block your time, you create a deficiency in your time management.

Calendar blocking is a strategy which completely revolutionized how I managed my time. It is the task of pre-planning and blocking your time in advance. I recommend you use a calendar with a monthly, weekly and a day view with 30 minute time blocks. In the daily view of your calendar, write down all of your non-negotiables, revenue generating activities and office hours. Schedule in your family time, church commitments, hair appointments and even your quiet time. Everything goes on your calendar.

Next "color block" your activities. Color blocking your calendar is life changing. I use highlighters to visually see how my time is divided. I can analyze by the colors if I am dividing my time efficiently to reach my goals. Any blank blocks of time can be used for other appointments and opportunities. Here is my color key:

Green - Revenue Generating Event or Appointment

Orange - Office Hours. This can be used for your job
if you still have a 9 to 5.

Yellow - Non-revenue generating appointment

Blue - Family and Fellowship Time

Pink - Personal Time

Purple - Prep Time

Time blocking is the queen of productivity. The mission is to eliminate distractions and increase productivity. Doing a time block, you turn off your phone, shut off your email and remove all other distractions. For a specified amount of uninterrupted time you focus on one singular goal. Don't switch between task. You lose time when your brain has to readjust. F.O.C.U.S. **F**ollow **O**ne **C**ourse **U**ntil **S**uccessful! There will be two main benefits. First, you will get more done in a short amount of time. Secondly, you will begin to have increased confidence in what you can do.

Time Management Hacks

Being a good steward of your time is often a learned behavior. Here are a few suggestions to help you be a better monitor of the 24 hours allotted to you daily.

1. Plan your week ahead of time. Including pick out your clothes, setting appointments and planning your menus.

2. Stop estimating the time you have to complete a task.

3. Schedule time for interruptions. Prepare for the unexpected.

4. Complete the biggest task first.

5. Schedule your tasks based on your energy surges during the day.

6. Use your time wisely making every minute count.

7. Eliminate time wasters (anything that is non productive in your life).

8. Create a to-do-list and cross off every accomplishment.

9. Celebrate when you reach a major milestone in your day.

10. Delegate or outsource.

11. Use technology to automate repetitive tasks.

12. Create an environment that suits your working style.

13. Pack your car at night.

Time waits for no one. It's the only asset that we have that we cannot recreate. There is a parable in the Good Book about ten virgins who were waiting for the bridegroom. No one knew the specific time of his arrival. In preparation they were given lamps with enough oil to find him when he called them to the wedding feast. Some virgins were frivolous with their supply and when the bridegroom came, their oil lamps were empty. They tried to borrow some, but it was too late. Don't be like the young virgins and not be prepared for your special opportunity. It may only knock once.

REVELATION 5

Being a Star Player is Nothing Without a Team

"Two are better than one; because they have
a good reward for their labour. For if they fall,
the one will lift up his fellow: but woe to
him that is alone when he falleth; for he hath
not another to help him up."
Ecclesiastes 4:9-10, KJV

You are the star player on your team. But every star player needs a team. You bring the intensity and build the foundation for your business. But you have to have a team that can work with you to help you win when it's time to play. On a daily basis, I do the work of many people. I'm often asked how do I do it without completely losing my mind. The answer is really simple, I don't do it all by myself. I have a first-class dream team. There's no way I could be an effective mother, wife, friend, daughter, business owner, consultant, housekeeper, chauffeur, mediator, or mentor without having someone to help me.

Everybody's dream team may look totally different. In the beginning, it may be just you and one other person. As your business grows, your team may grow to hundreds maybe even thousands but your dream team will have to be constructed around your needs, your strengths and even your weaknesses. Your team should be there for you on a personal and a professional basis. Sometimes these two groups may crossover, but very rarely. Just like a personal life and a business life, you need a personal dream team and a business dream team. It is important to have great expectations for both. Be clear on what they should expect from you and what you should expect from them.

My personal dream team holds me up and support me in everything. They are my friends and my family. They are people that I can have watch my children, pray for me or even have a night out on-the-town with. They are my inner circle. These are people who directly support me. Now, people who directly support me may not support my business, but without them in a supporting role, I cannot be fully available for my business.

Then I have my professional dream team. These are people who assist me in the day-to-day operations of my business. These are people who are my realtor, my accountant, my web designers, my mastermind group, my marketing director and my stylist. These are people who directly support the business and the brand of *The Millionaire Midwife*.

So many of you are probably thinking well, how do I create a dream team? You know a lot of people who already faithfully support you. Talk to them intentionally about how you can place them on your team. Don't overlook your supporters. All supporters may not have the skills that you're looking for, but these are people that have the will and passion to assist you. These are the people that are going to help you in the middle of the night prepare for the event. They will read a copy of your book before you even publish it. They're going to give you the raw truth about matters that are close to your heart.

In my first year of opening my school, Imagine Me Academy, I got about 20 volunteers and these are the people that I could call on at any time to do anything. They were not on the payroll then, but four of them are now on my paid dream team. They have the skills and the will to help and they all played a significant role in the school's success.

Identify areas that are causing you the most stress and taking up your time. Find someone to help you or do them for you. Remember, you're looking for people who can help you consistently and continuously. These are great positions for your dream team. These people may be in your inner circle or you may even need to find someone new. They can make your life easier and eliminate the unnecessary stresses. When I hired a social media manager, my life changed for the better. It wasn't something that I needed because I didn't have the skill, but it was the thing that was taking up so much of my time that I could have been using to generate income.

Communicating is truly the secret weapon for effective teams. Consider how you're going to communicate your vision and their individual roles to each of your team members. Effective communication is the true sign of an effective leader. Make sure that you have a written vision, it helps people to understand where you're going. Efficiently communicate the vision and why it needs to be accomplished. The people on your team should be able to communicate and relate to that vision and your core principles to run this race with you. You need to surround yourself with people who can.

Understand that not all people will be able to carry the vision that you have because God has not ordained them to be in your circle. It's okay! Everybody won't be able to carry this baby with you, it's your baby. But there will be people along the way that can help you. You need to be able to detect the doubters versus the doers, the non-believers versus the believers. You will have people that want to help, and others that just want to spectate. Move the spectators off of your team as quick as possible. "Don't bring a big goal to small-minded people." This will be important to maintain the engagement of your team and to keep them encouraged and hopeful. You will also need to have mentors in the background to gird you and your team up along the way. Even though I believe I am a great mentor, midwife, and business owner, I need mentors and advisers as well. Starting a business, doing great on your job or even being a great family member sometimes takes the wisdom of someone else who has walked on a similar pathway before you. Acquiring a mentor or adviser does not have to be complicated or expensive. Yet, you do need someone who can see ahead of you and give you great sound advice. In the beginning, I had a lot of questions. I sought out people that I never met because they knew what I had to know in order to prosper. I listened to their information and implemented accordingly. I was able to get a mentor that was able to help me walk through my dream. This journey of entrepreneurship does not have to be lonely. You have to create a system along the way that supports you personally and professionally.

What should you do with your dream team? Make sure you are utilizing them to their greatest potential, but you also want to make sure that their relationship with you is fair and also beneficial to them. In the beginning, you may not be able to pay everyone on your team, but there are different ways that you can compensate people. As your business grows, I really encourage you to turn your dream team into your dream employees.

How do you delegate to elevate? You need to begin to delegate. Delegation is the process of authorizing people to represent you. You're literally entrusting them with an important task. There cannot be any entrusting where there is no trust. So over time you need to test and try relationships before delivering large projects to people that you don't know or you haven't worked with.

There are several questions you can answer to decide if the delegation of a certain task is right for you.

1. Is it a low pay grade task?

2. Does this task directly bring revenue in the business?

3. Can I create a simple system for someone else to complete this task?

4. How time consuming is this task? If I can do it in 5 - 15 minutes. I don't delegate. The exception is for repeated tasks like data entry or customer service.

5. Will delegating this task help increase my productivity and profits?

You need to make sure that you're delegating functions that allow you to create income in your business. All the tasks that you would consider a minimum wage or low-grade salary should be delegated. If you're valuing your services at $100 an hour, why are you doing the minimum wage job in your business? What do I mean by that? You can't be labeling all the folders in your office. You should not be making every service call, do inventory or type every email. These are things that people on your dream team can have delegated to them. There are some service oriented tasks, like follow-ups, implementation calls, or customer calls that you may want to delegate to people who you know have great customer service skills. This extra measure will make your customers feel extra special, but protect your time. Delegations also give you a little buffer between your customers and yourself.

There is a huge difference between being self-employed and a business owner. Your business must be able to operate without you. If people only trust you and you're the only face that they want to see, you're going to wear yourself out. We've talked a lot in this book about the fact that you have a limited amount of time and energy. You can maximize your time and energy through delegation. One of the methods I use when I'm delegating is I ask myself if the task is bringing money directly into the business? A lot of times I handle these tasks, especially if it's supporting the business. If it's not directly bringing in money, these are things that I delegate.

This is a great rule of thumb for you to use when you are delegating: One, why is this job a low pay grade task? Not that it's not important, but is it a low pay grade task? Two, is it a task that brings money directly into the business? If it is a very low pay grade task and it does not bring money directly into the business, this is a great way to decide if you should outsource. Another thing to consider is how time consuming is it? So, tasks that would take more than three hours are tasks that I always consider delegating. If I can set up the system to get it done in those three hours by someone else, I can use those hours for an income generating activity.

Outsourcing is a form of delegating. You're delegating to people who do not work directly for you. It may be a person or a consultant who may have their own business. It could be a virtual assistant or it can be someone on a website like Upwork or Fiverr. These people are experts in helping small business owners and large corporations. They can do things as small as answering the phone for you or as large as setting up a call center that is able to answer hundreds of calls an hour. These outsourcing companies allow you to get the job done without the liability of training, onboarding, and staffing a host of employees that you may only need temporarily or for short-term assignments. Outsourcing may be used to get a project up and running. Outsourcing is great on things that are specialized like editing, website design or graphic design.

I love outsourcing tasks with a specialized project because I'm going to get a different viewpoint than with my internal team. Another reason to outsource is to get a different set of eyes on your business or on your project.

As you're growing your business consider the people, you need on your dream team. You don't have to be an army of one. Consider how you will delegate and outsource to control the amount of money and time it takes to accomplish a task. Having a dream team is a huge part of my success. I cannot do it alone. In fact, my dreams are so much bigger than me. I would have gone crazy trying to be a one woman show. My dreams just aren't designed like that. I am sincerely grateful for all of the people who have supported my dreams over the years. This journey of entrepreneurship definitely becomes real with a supporting cast. All of you can be the star player you dream of. Make sure that you have a supporting team to support you along the way.

REVELATION 6

Clarity = Cash

And the LORD answered me, and said,
Write the vision, and make it plain upon tablets,
that he may run that readeth it. For the vision is
yet for an appointed time, but at the end it shall speak,
and not lie: though it tarry, wait for it; because it
will surely come, it will not tarry.
Habakkuk 2:2 - 3, KJV.

Clarity equals cash, there is no doubt about it. This concept is the connection between how clear you are about your business and the cash flow you should expect. The less clear you are, the less cash you will generate in your business. As this clarity increases, you will see your revenue, your cash flow and your customer attraction will sky rocket.

The clarity part of "clarity equals cash" includes you getting clear about both your business goals and your life goals. So the first thing that you need to do as an individual is to be very clear about what you want out of life. There's no sense in committing to goals that do not align with your purpose. Once you know your goals, you can develop focus and discipline. The less focused you are in your business, the less cash you will generate.

Clearing Out the Clutter

If you know that you want to be a stay at home mom, but you're thinking about a business that's going to cause you to travel weekly, it's not going to work. Your personal goal and your career goal would not be aligned. The same dynamic comes into play when your personal and your career goals are not being aligned to your spiritual goals. There will always be a conflict between what you want to do, what you can do and what you will do. Getting clear about your goals is the initial key to your success. Sometimes we wonder, "Should I really do this?" If we sit back and analyze the way we want our life to look, the answer will come easily.

Clarity Activities

The following activity will give you a defined vision of what you want in life. Don't deceive yourself. Don't think that something is too small or too big. This is the time for you to wake up every personal aspiration, every dormant hope and every delayed dream. Prepare yourself for increase. See yourself past today. Once your vision is clear, create a plan to get you there. Your plan is the fuel that will get your engine roaring to takeoff.

To increase clarity about your life, complete these effective clarity exercises.

Activity I: *Vision Your Future*

Vision Your Future is a great way to get all those beautiful ideas out of your head and heart and on paper. Just writing down your aspirations give your self-conscious mind permission to succeed. This will be a great experience.

1. Grab fresh a notebook.

2. Sit down and really take an assessment of where you are right now. Just write don't censor yourself. Explore what you want to change and what you want to keep. Think about different areas of your life: social, emotional, career, spiritual, health and finance are just some possible areas you may want to explore.

3. Describe where you see yourself in 5 years, 10 years and 20 years. What do you want your life to look like? You can use the same categories: social, emotional, career, spiritual, health and finance and any other areas you fill you need to explore. Once you decide how you want your life to look, you can move towards building the kind of business you

want to have that can afford you the life you desire. Many people overestimate what they can do in one year but underestimate the transformation they can have in ten years. If you use your time and resources wisely, you can have the life you desire and more. We serve a God that can do exceedingly abundantly above what we can ask or think. (Ephesians 3:20)

Activity II: *What's for me?*

What's for me? is a great activity that has help my clients and myself decide the correct course of action. As creatives and entrepreneur, we often have a host of aspirations. This activity is designed to help you answer the age old question, "What's for me?" Warning: this activity is not meant to limit you in any way. It will help you prioritize and see time and opportunity differently. Let's go!

1. List out everything you want to do. Be liberal! It could be acquiring a certain amount of income, writing a book or starting a fashion line. No matter what it is you want to accomplish, put it down on paper.

2 Break your list up into four sections:

    A. Things you accomplish within a month (Examples: Write an article. Make a commercial. Start a blog, vlog or YouTube Channel. Host a workshop.)

B. Things you accomplish do within a quarter (Example: Start a support group for battered women. Write a book. Start coaching service.)

C. Things you accomplish in a year (Example: Open a daycare! Grow your email list to 10,000.)

D. Things you can accomplish in a year or more. (Speak at Essence. Learn a new marketable skill like website design. Learn a new language. Become debt free.)

3. Cross out anything that you are not truly passionate about. This is going to help you decide what to focus on now bringing clarity to how you should spend your resources.

Time is money. If you waste your time, you're not going to get it back. You also waste the opportunity to do the things that generate revenue and bring you closer to your vision for your life.

Activity III: *Thinking of a Master Plan*

Not that you've decided what you are going to focus on, it's time to create your master plan. *Thinking of a Master Plan* is a very important activity. Your plan and rate of consistency you execute your plan is also paramount. Real execution and focus are required to achieve your goals.

You're going to have to ask yourself several questions to construct a solid plan to see your goals become a reality.

1. Why are you going after this goal?

2. What do you hope to gain from it? (Personally and Professionally)

3. Does it have a monetary reward?

4. Who will benefit if you accomplish this goal?

5. If applicable, how much will people pay for your service or product?

6. What resources do you need to do to make this goal a reality?

7. Who/what do you need to help you accomplish this goal?

8. What is your timeframe for completing this goal?

9. If you don't accomplish this goal what consequence will you experience?

10. Who can mentor you in accomplishing these goals?

Once you answer these questions, you can construct a detailed plan to bring your dream to reality. Once clarity becomes a reality, it can become a cash cow. Often times because we haven't fully considered our goals and constructed a plan, we simply fail to pursue wholeheartedly. We are great at starting. In creating a step-by-step plan, we are more likely to make the progress needed to be a finisher.

Activity IV: *Vision and Profit Boards*

Vision Board have become quite popular over the years. You may see them as a kid like activity to cut-and-paste pictures and words on a poster board. I assure you this process is effective and motivating. We need to physically develop a tangible vision for what kind of life you want. Vision boards can be a collection of photos, affirmations, or words that keep your vision front and center. A few years ago, I also began to develop a Profit Board. The profit board connected the vision for my life to the monetary gain I was expecting. I added ways that I would generate income and my revenue goals. In fact, I began to declare through my board and through affirmations that money and opportunities to generate wealth was unlimited and on its way to me, NOW!

Vision and Profit Boards are living and breathing visual that changes and grows with you. You will be amazed as your intentions begin to manifest. You can change your vision board as often as you like. I recommend you redesign your vision board at least once a year to be a relevant source of inspiration and motivation.

REVELATION 7

Profiting from Your Pain

God, your God, will restore everything you lost;
he'll have compassion on you; he'll come back
and pick up the pieces from all the places
where you were scattered.

Deuteronomy 30:3 MSG

Profiting from your pain, may be one of the most en-
lightening Revelations in this book for two reasons.
One, the birthing of your purpose may be a result of a painful
situation. Two, learning to embrace your pain may turn difficult times into rewarding times. If that tragedy did not happen to you, you may have never come up with that money-sav-
ing idea or have compassion for people in the same situation.
I'm going to give you an example of how I learned from my personal pain. It was very detrimental when it was happening, but

later it became the reason for opening my chain of private schools. When my daughter was a toddler, we sought help because she had a difficult time accumulating at school. She was very uncomfortable. She cried often, found it difficult to make friends and was at times overly aggressive. We were very concerned about her emotional and mental state. Every school that we put her in, we had problems because they struggled to care for her. It was truly difficult to see her struggle. Eventually, I decided to open my own school so that children like my daughter could get the education and help they deserved. There were limited facilities in our area that accepted children with physical emotional or behavioral challenges or would take the risk of caring for kids with "special needs." When I decided to open up my own school, my main goal was to provide a safe educational haven for children and their parents who wrestled with broken school systems and limited choices. I admitted EVERY child even if it was a child that had a lot of challenges and a disability. We were committed to helping each child by working parents, therapist and special accommodations to make the experience at *Imagine Me Academy* positive. When I started my school, I built an atmosphere where we implemented caring conflict resolution. I based this decision on the fact that children that have emotional and physical challenges need structure, guidance and love. Our staff was deliberately composed of people that could help children and love them at the same time.

I built this environment, in a very small community. I decided that I was not going to give up on any child.

If I didn't have the personal experience with my own daughter, I wouldn't have known this type of facility needed to exist. We give them the best support that we can, so children with special needs can adequately function in a learning environment. We are the solution I prayed for and that solution became my greatest blessing. As a result, people in the community began to know us for something different, they knew us as a safe refuge, a school that offered great academics and a loving environment. Over the years, we gained a lot of experience. My business acumen kicked in and we began to grow. After turning my personal pain into a million dollar empire, I felt called to help other entrepreneurs do the same. Coaching other people on how to be effective as an entrepreneur and starting their own businesses is one of my greatest joys. I have the ability to take complex tasks and break them down in a way that it is obtainable and digestible.

You need to ask yourself, what am I good at? What are those pain points that you wish you could change? What can be a viable solution for your pain? There is a population who may have the same problem and you can be a solution for them. If you have the answer to people's problems, it will always provide an income for you. It could come by the way of money, donations, building a platform; but it will definitely profit you in the end.

Life Experiences

Now is the time for you to put the pain aside and do a personal inventory. Revisit some of those painful experiences but this time look for the treasure in each trial. Ask yourself, what am I naturally good at? What are some things that I do well? What are the things that people always compliment me on? How can I use those skills, gifts, and talents? What are the things that I do naturally that other people struggle with? How can I use that to further promote me in business? How can I use those skills to create a business and do it with ease? Once we answer these questions, you will begin to identify how you can be a solution in the marketplace. When your business is connected to something you truly love, it doesn't even seem like work. This is the reason that I've made hundreds of thousands of dollars training people all across this nation. The ability to take a concept and create a business model for someone makes me feel like a kid in a candy store.

Zone of Genius

What is it that you can do that other people find difficult? This is your zone of genius. Your zone of genius is the area where you are highly skilled and proficient. I know that in my heart of hearts, all of these skills that I have attained in all of the places that I was successful and those where I was not, helps me to be

The Millionaire Midwife. My zone of genius is to help businesses boom. I know God has revealed to me a business model for abundant wealth.

Business management is my zone of genius. I know how to manage employees, obtain Government contracts and operate Federal programs. I've had the pleasure to work with non-profit as well as for-profit companies. The experiences I've had allowed me to create a model to be a successful entrepreneur. God allowed me to work in different leadership positions, over 30 schools and over 300 employees before I was a business owner. It was the lessons that I learned during this time that sustained me in my own company. Things that you're great at doing should not be abandoned despite the trials and tribulations that we experience in life. Take your time and reflect over your life and find out what is your true purpose as an entrepreneur. If you are able to do things that other people find difficult, this is where your riches lie. When God gives you a vision for your business, He will provide the experiences and make you into the kind of entrepreneur He wants you to be. He creates compassion, resilience and ideas that will propel you to an expected end.

REVELATION 8

Connect, Cultivate & Cash Out

Wealth gained by dishonesty will be diminished,

but he who gathers by labor will increase.

Proverbs 13:11, KJV.

The connect, cultivate and cash out model is a three-dimensional approach to ensure profitability in your business. This model was birthed through trial and error and many successes and failures in my business and those of my business associates. The three-tiered model mirrors a business funnel often used in the sales world. In a sales funnel you move people from prospect to paying customer.

Connect

Your business plan is actually the center of your business operation, but it doesn't always prepare you for the human connection, clients and/or customers you need for your business to grow. How do you connect with your customer? From the onset of meeting you, the potential customer forms an opinion about you and what you are bringing to the table. Their *What's In It For Me* is at the forefront of their minds. A person may meet you but may not have decided what kind of relationship they want to have with you. They won't do that until they know how it's going to benefit them. Making a good first impression is uber important. Most researchers say that you have 30 seconds or less to impress someone. Your body language, tone, personality and word choice help people determine if they want to build a relationship with you. In today's time, our first introduction to people is often virtual. As entrepreneurs, we have to be very aware of our digital footprint. New contacts could be connecting with you on social media, via your website, phone call, webinar, or even through television. The initial point of connection is the medium that drives them to you and vice versa. This initial connection will often make or break the relationship. It is important to add value in every setting. Some examples of adding value is giving vital information, encouragement, or providing a new connection. As you meet new people make sure you begin to build your army of collaborators, affiliates and community by building your own database of contacts. Although building a social media following is important, I caution every entrepreneur for being responsible for maintaining their own contacts. In the connection phase you will attract many, but in the cultivation phase, you will find your true following.

Cultivating

Cultivating and nurturing relationships it once its established is very important. Introducing people to your brand and making them a part of your online community should be one of your initial goals to their query about your services or products. But, when do you really know that you have a qualified client or customer or business prospect? When contacts begin to seriously consider your services or products, they will engage you in such a way that you know they are interested in working with you. For example, they may buy a low-cost product or join a free challenge. They will begin to look forward to receiving information from you and sign up for your newsletter. There are several ways to cultivate prospects online and offline and convert them to buyers:

1. Email Marketing

2. Webinars

3. eBooks

4. Thank You Cards

5. Challenges

6. Social Media Groups (Facebook and LinkedIn)

7. Live Stream

8. Free Consultation

9. Beta Product or Service Trials

10. Events

11. Masterminds

12. Social Causes

Cashing Out

"Cashing Out" is my favorite component and this sentiment is shared by most business owners! This is what we work tirelessly to do. Our ultimate goal is to turn that connection into CASH. Remember, nothing happens until a sale takes place. One of my frequently asked questions is: Brandy how long should I stay in the connect or cultivate phase before I actually cash out? And the answer to this is easy, it depends. This is not the answer you may want to hear. Right? People take different amounts of time to connect with you. It also depends on what your business model is and if you sell products or a service. Let's say, you sell candles, and your customer comes to you to buy candles, your connection and cash out may happen within minutes. If they like your brand, they like your honesty, and you connect in a relatively short time. You cultivate the relationship and show them products they love and they may buy the candle, within 15-minutes. You have gone through all these processes. This is not a reasonable timeline for a sale that requires a substantial investment or you nurturing a trusting relationship. For example, in the real estate industry this process can take 3-6 months before they connect, cultivate and cash out with a client. The agent must find out what kind of houses they like, their preferences, and financially what they can afford. Once a selection is made, they go through the closing. This process could take numerous months or over a year. The length of the process in your industry has a lot to do with when you may cash out.

Don't be dismayed by how long it takes to catch a big fish. You're out there grinding and people are watching you. Just do good work and be consistent. They may not be ready to make a purchase now, but someday they will be interested and ready to buy. In an instant, they may decide to become your next million-dollar client because you connected, cultivated and now it's your turn to cash out.

Concise Marketing

Let's dig a little deeper, how do you use marketing to connect? You need to know who your ideal customer is. I believe everybody should decide who their ideal customer is in the beginning of their business start-up. I have to be honest, I have multiple customer profiles in my business. For *Imagine Me Academy*, my chain of schools an ideal parent is a full-time working parent. They want the best for their child academically and desire a nurturing and loving environment. They connect with the school and its mission. They don't want to pay extravagant tuition and fees, but they are not bargain shopping either. Since I know who my customer is, all of my marketing is designed to attract them and address a pain point or answer a question about our services. That doesn't mean I won't get a parent who is still in college, or who is a stay-at-home mom. However, the majority of the parents who are interested in my school are ideal customers and my marketing and services speak to them. Every time I promote my business, my marketing is targeting my ideal customer. 90% of the time the mother makes the decision about childcare. I'm not talking to the father in my marketing. I speak to that mother who wants to be sure their pride and joy is being well cared for in a safe environment. Knowing your ideal customer will help you face the next stage of connecting, cultivating and cashing out. You need to consider your marketing strategy in everything you do to promote your business. It includes your logo, messaging, brand colors, the type of program you offer and your pricing. Your marketing strategy will tell you how to reach and retain your ideal customer. Every aspect of your marketing needs to speak directly to your ideal customer. Interviewing your ideal customer is going to help you when you get to the marketing phase of your business. Take time and survey a minimum of 100 people that you consider your ideal customer. Use the information you gather to create ad copy, emails, graphics and other promotional strategies to attract them. This will save you time and money. Effective marketing will help you reach your ideal customer and cash out quickly. Concise marketing and branding puts the eyes of your ideal client on you and keeps them there.

Power Closing

Since you have connected and cultivated that relationship, it is up to you to close the deal! It's time to CASH OUT! Your job is to move them from a prospect to a paying customer. These are some ways to close the sale:

1. Listen to what your prospect is telling you. Don't bring obstacles into the conversation.

2. In listening, be slow to speak. Allow the quiet time for your prospect to speak and don't be afraid to talk while you are closing. Don't be afraid to allow them time to react to your questions.

3. Always assume the sale. You're not going to ask for it, assume you already have it. Ask questions like: "When do you want to get started?" "Where would you like me to send your welcome package?"

4. You need to know how to overcome objections. Most of the time, when you don't close on a business deal, people are going to give you, 4-6 objections. You must find out what those objections are and find 2-3 ways to overcome them. Remember, a confused mind won't buy.

5. Always have your contract available with pen in hand. If it is a product, be stocked and ready to deliver.

6. Once the deal is done, collect your funds. Make sure you have payment methods that are easy and hassle-free.

The Fortune is In the Follow-Up

What happens if people don't buy? The magic is in the follow-up. Sometimes, a "no" today, is a "yes" tomorrow. One of the biggest reasons people don't win is 48% of entrepreneurs don't follow-up. Research says only 25% of sales representatives follow up one or two times, 12% follow-up three times and only 10% will follow up more than three times. Please don't leave money on the table by not following up. You must realize 80% of all sales happen between the 5th and the 12th contact. Be the 10% that make 80% of the sales. Follow-up can be the bulk of your revenue. I have a 2-day, a 2-week and a 2-month-old follow-up strategy. Initially, I will ask for the sale. If they need to think about it, I'll give them 2-days before contacting them again. If we are in constant communication, I will talk to them every two days. If not,

I will wait 2-weeks to follow-up. During that time, I gather all the information asked for and attempt to add value by cultivating the relationship. Sometimes there is even a longer delay in converting a prospect to a customer. No matter what, I will follow-up in 2 months to re-engage and see if they are ready. Being persistent will definitely increase your chance of closing the sale. I'm going to push. Even if I get a firm "no," I am going to be professional in following up. Referrals and other opportunities can present themselves from cultivating relationships through follow-up. Remember, you can follow up with people in many ways. You can call, email, or text. Your goal is to get the sale. It may take some time. But with proper follow-up, I guarantee, you will cash out more often. Cha-ching!

REVELATION 9

Money is Everywhere

Lazy hands make for poverty,
but diligent hands bring wealth.
Proverbs 10:4, NIV

We can't deny that money is everywhere. Money attracts money! The truth is lazy hands make for poverty, but diligent hands bring wealth. The way you attract or repel money is connected to your belief about money. Your money mindset will either make you a money magnet or money repellent.

Money is actually repelled by desperation. The more desperate you are for money, the harder it is to come by. However, if you know the rules of financial reciprocity and the monetary principles associated with money, you can definitely attract as much moolah as you want.

In this Revelation, I will discuss ways to generate income and wealth. There are so many ways that you can make tons of cash and accumulate wealth. Everyone, including me, wishes that they had a rich uncle or family that they were born into, but the truth of the matter is there's a small percentage of people that are actually born into wealth. Most millionaires that you see are actually self-made. What sets them apart? What would set you apart from the average person if you were to become a millionaire? Let's investigate!

On a Biblical Note

You manifest what you believe (as a man thinketh, so is he - see Proverbs 23:7). If you believe you're poor, struggling, just getting by, or barely making ends meet, that is exactly what you will receive. If you believe that you are more than a conqueror, you will be. You will never hear me pray the prayer "God, meet my needs," because that is not my desire. My desire is that God will bless me above my needs, and I will overflow in abundance and there will not be enough room for me to receive all of it (see Malachi 3:10).

There are two principles you must understand about manifestation. First of all, whatever you think and whatever you believe, that is what it is going to be. Secondly, whatever you're praying for, or whatever you believe in your heart, that is what you're going to receive. God is a God that answers prayers. He's going to meet that need. If you're praying for abundance and super abundance, you will receive just that. Hold fast the promise that He gives seed to the sower. Sow knowing you are expecting a great harvest. Sow in your business. Sow in your dreams. If you believe that He's going to give you the power to get wealth, and that money answers all things, that's what you're going to receive.

Recently, I had a true revelation from God, *"Being Broke Ain't Biblical."* As I was speaking to a crowd, the words flowed freely from my mouth. It was a Rhema word. According to Deuteronomy 8:18, God has given us the ability to get wealth. So why are we operating in lack? There is no reason to walk in lack when God has called us to a wealthy place.

How to Generate Money

There are many ways to make money. The most common three are active, residual, and passive income. Active income is money that you work for. Basically, you are trading dollars for hours. Active income is the pay you receive working on your job or your profits in your business. It can come in many different ways, whether you're getting paid hourly, being paid a salary or commission.

Entrepreneurs make active income when they make a sale that could be $100, $1,000, or $10,000 based on the cost of the service or product. They can calculate how much income they've made based on their active sales.

Active income is the earnings directly worked for. It's what we consider as a daily grind. It is what you're putting your time and your energy towards on a daily basis that causes income to come into your home or causes revenue to come into your business. This is the money you have to work for and this is the main way that most people make their money. The more you work, the more you make. The problem with active income is you only have a limited amount of time and energy. When you stop so does the coins! Can you imagine building a million-dollar business this way? No. Most wealthy people do not make their money working for active income alone.

With active income, you work for it every single day. What happens when you are exhausted and can't go anymore? You're out of income! What happens if you get sick? Your money stops! What happens when you don't have customers in a day, a week or even a month? There are no bank deposits. So, this income is exclusively based on your sales market, ability, time, and your energy.

The next type of income is residual income. This is by far one of my favorite types of income. This is where we talk about compound interest. It's the type of interest that gives you exponential results. There's also compound effort, meaning the effort I put in today can also give me some results later. So, I work today, I receive money on that work later on and I'm going to keep receiving money from the work that I have already done. That is the good life! It could be in the form of commission sales, interest on a particular investment, income from rental property, or repeat customers. Residual income can also come from you having other people working in your organization that's going to bring you more income such as multi-level marketing, franchises, and financial dividends.

Residual and passive income have some common attributes. They almost look like twins, but they're not identical twins. Passive income is income that you're not working for anymore. A great example of passive income is income from Internet sales. It can also come from systems that you have in place where you receive a commission anytime you sell a particular item or product. Passive income could come from online courses, drop shipping, affiliate marketing, or a unique system that you created where people buy goods and services.

A membership site is a great example of passive income. You build the program one member at a time. No matter if one person or one million people subscribe, your investment is the same. Once you breakeven, everything else is passive income. This is how you can experience explosive wealth. You are no longer trading dollars for hours. Anyone that comes in through that program creates more passive income for you.

Combining Income Types

The magic happens when you learn how to make money using all three income streams simultaneously. There are many ways to convert your active income into passive or residual income.

Let's look at these two scenarios.

As entrepreneurs, we must build a solid following and should work diligently on building our email list in addition to a social media following. That first time someone buys a product or service, you have actively converted them from a window shopper to a customer. This is active income.

Now this customer is on your email list. You own the contact, unlike on social media where they can shutdown your account down without warning. You continue to cultivate them (and thousands of others) and they buy your book and attend one of your paid master classes. You are on a roll. Passively you are making money from your efforts.

This customer now becomes an ambassador for your brand. They join your affiliate market program and begin to sell your products or services for a commission. You have just entered a residual income loop by bringing in revenue based on someone else's efforts.

When you think about money coming to you, you either make money actively through your direct effort or you're going to make it from the relationships that you establish, passive or residual income. The system has already set the pace and people just plug into it without even realizing it sometimes. We call this an evergreen system. They work effortlessly around the clock. An evergreen system is a strategic combination of people, processes, and technology to deliver optimal results. Your job is to market and send potential clients in the right direction. All you need to do is prepare yourself for a 6-figure or a 7-figure income by sending customers through your system that continues to pay you when you are sleep.

Recently, I have been following a newer urban makeup brand out of New Orleans that started in 2017. The brand was born to be a cash cow. The marketing strategy appealed to make-up artists, everyday divas and developed a social media presence that has grown to over 1.5 million followers on the business and CEO's Instagram page. She is attracting money daily with her efforts being compounded by brand ambassadors. They continue to sell out of any promotional offer. They actively promote new products through ads, trade shows and several distribution channels. Passive revenue on this brand makes money from reorders, bundles and up. I have been a victim more than once. They have closed the income loop by making residual sales from make-up artists and wholesale distribution. This is a great example of how these types of incomes can work together to generate wealth in a short amount of time. Always have an open mind and an open heart believing that everything that belongs to you is on its way to you. Build the business that draws money to you. Every single day you must be positive about your monetary flow. Money is about attitude and mindset, more than the products or services you sell.

The Law of Large Numbers

The Law of Large Number is a mathematical principle that changed my life. You cannot depend on a few customers to bring you wealth. You need to be talking to a large amount of people every day actively face-to-face, online or via social media to get the customers you want to make your money actively or passively.

At any given time, only 3% of people are ready to buy what you are selling. So in order to make the amount of sales you need to reach your goal, you need to connect with more people. The more people you reach, the more customers you will convert. Remember, money is everywhere and the money that belongs to you will come to you! Believe it and receive it, now!

REVELATION 10

Compounding Efforts

And whatsoever ye do, do it heartily,
as to the Lord, and not unto men;...
Colossians 3:23, KJV

Many people are curious about the success of people that they admire. Success is broken down into three areas: duplication, scaling and compounding results. Duplication is the idea that you are able to duplicate yourself in the organizations, businesses, and ministries that you are involved in. By teaching others to the skills that you have, you are literally cloning yourself. Think about the things that you do daily in your business. Are you the only person doing these tasks? If so, this may be an instructional element that you can share with others. Remember when I talked with you about your having a finite amount of time and energy? In order to really be successful, you have to begin to duplicate yourself.

Now don't get me wrong, one person probably cannot do everything that you can. I focus on creating a team of people that are able to run your business, nonprofit organization without you, you win. It's almost like having a small town where you are mayor. You are surrounded by others just like you every day. People that you have taught to think like you, to carry the vision like you, and who can also succeed like you do. It's really impacting when you add experts in particular areas. When you start a business, you need a success plan. This plan is a monument to your success. Whenever you decide to walk away, to leave and do something greater than what you've built, it doesn't die. It can live and continue. That cannot happen without duplication. Another way you may duplicate is franchising. Franchising is duplication on steroids. Everyone who passes through your doors will recognize your brand. Business can be influenced geographically, but having a popular product works everywhere. "Two all-beef patties, special sauce, lettuce, cheese, pickles, onions, on a sesame seed bun," you know the song. It doesn't matter if they are in California, New York, Idaho, you can walk into any McDonald's and get the same Big Mac. Why? Because their system is duplicatable. I read that your business should not depend on people. Your business should depend on positions. Granted, you must have the right people to fill those positions. Think back to McDonald's, which positions do you see at each store that allows them to run efficiently? You have a front counter clerk, drive-thru attendant, fry cook, sandwich maker, and managers. Without someone in each position, the system fails. But within a day or two, you can train someone to fill those positions. Now, consider your organization. What positions are needed to make your business flourish? Are those positions well thought out? Do you have the systems in place to train people for each position? No matter how much you love your employees, people will not stay with you forever. You need to be able to cross train people in numerous positions. Seriously, it doesn't matter if Frank, Ciara or Sarah is on the clock, what does matter is that their position is filled by a qualified individual. You need to know what works for your business and duplicate those processes and positions. When you are able to duplicate, you are able to expand. Where there is expansion, there is increased revenue. Every time you are able to duplicate yourself create a well-defined position or a system within your business, you're setting yourself up for bigger revenue.

Scaling

The word scaling in business is a little different from what we think about naturally. When I first heard the phrase "scaling up," I wondered about its meaning. I knew you could grow your business' size, but scaling is not just growth. Scaling is your ability to multiply your revenue with minimal incremental costs. You are growing your business, but not spending tons of cash to do so. In typical growth models when revenue increases, your costs increase. This is not the case with scaling. So how does that work? You need to know your capacity to handle additional business growth and be confident in how you manage your business and its processes. Scaling can be difficult in service-oriented business. If you are providing a service like marketing or website design, scaling may be a challenge unless you can replicate your effects using technology. A lot of times you can see scaling in businesses with products. With a little creativity, you can do it in service or product-based businesses. For example, let's say you created a software or app. Once a software and app is created, you can sell it multiple times with minimal maintenance or cost over and over again. Also, products like vitamins can be reproduced millions of times without changing the formula. The initial investment may be substantial, but the reproduction happens at a minimal cost. The same thing goes for producers of CDs, once that recordings are done, the artist produces that CD, they can duplicate that CD over and over again and sell it as many times as they want. These models are very scalable because they are products. However, if you have a business that is a service it may be a little more challenging. For example, in the childcare industry you are trading dollars for hours. I'm going to take care of your child and you're going to pay me this amount. This base cost does not change. One way you can scale this business is to have a larger building where you can offset your overhead. You can use systems to automate tasks to reduce labor cost. You can also add supplemental services or products to increase revenue in your service pool. Lastly, you can open multiple centers that use the same proven model, saving tons of time and money while increasing your overall customer base. As you can see, in the service industry it's a little bit more difficult to scale. But it's doable. This is how I have made my fortune!

I want you to think about the mighty Walmart of the world. If you went into a Walmart 10 years ago, you would see 20 cashiers in the front of the building and they were all ready to serve you. Now, if you go into Walmart, you're going to see 20 self-service registers and maybe 2 or 3 cashiers. They figured out a way to reduce costs and labor in order to scale their business model. Another way they've scaled their business is by adding more and more stores. Using technology, they added online services where you can order products and they are sent directly to you or they provide easy pickup at the store. Using ingenuity, Walmart has stayed current with the times and consistently delivers premium customer satisfaction while raking up billions in revenue each year. Think outside of the box. Here are some questions you can ask yourself:

1. How can your customers schedule their service with you automatically?

2. How can customers receive their goods and services from you automatically?

3. How can you reduce cost while your revenue increases?

4. What aspects of your business can you outsource?

5. How can you increase the number of distribution avenues?

6. How can I reduce labor cost?

We don't just want to grow, we want to scale! With automation, outsourcing and increasing the use of technology in our business, we can keep our focus on attracting more customers. Remember, growth is where our revenue and our expenses grow at the same rate, but with scaling our revenue grows while our cost stays very, very low.

Compounding Results

You can increase your income is with compounding results. This is actually the secret super weapon of successful entrepreneurs. If you can learn this, you will find yourself in a better position than most. So what is compounding results? You probably have heard of compounding interest. It is the idea that not only your money grows, but the interest grows on your money. Einstein called it the 8th wonder of the world. So every year you are receiving more and more money, not because you keep investing, but you are receiving more interest on the actual interest. That's dope!

Let's take that same idea and think about compounding your results or efforts. I was once asked this question: "Would you rather get one million dollars today or would you rather get one penny and it doubles every day for 30 days?" I had to think about the question because I knew there was a catch. I have to tell you, I wanted to say, "Hey give me my million dollars and I will figure out the rest." I forced myself to think for a minute because I knew a little about compounding interest. I said: Well let me think about it." I did a little calculation and I am so glad that I didn't answer quickly. I tell you what, I will take that penny that doubles every day. This is how it works: if you take a penny a day, on day 2 yeah you only have 2 cents, day 3 you have 4 cents and it keeps going on and on, but after about 10 days, you will have 5 dollars, then you have 10 dollars, then 20, then 40, etc. When you get to your 30th day, believe it or not, you would have $5,368,709.12 and if it was a 31-day month, you would have $10,737,418.24. Talk about the compound effort! A lot of you think there is something called an 'overnight success', but it is just not true. People you see on your TV screen, topping the charts, onstage or on the New York Times Best Seller List have been busting their butts. You may wonder where they came from. I can guarantee you they've been working in the background, sometimes in their garages, at hole in the wall clubs, or at small conferences for years to get where they are. Now they are receiving the recognition for all the hard work they did for pennies and now they are finally cashing their six and seven figure checks. I'm not a scientist, but one of the things that's always impacted me was Newton's First Law of Motion. It basically says things in motion, stay in motion, but things at rest, stay at rest. Are you at rest or are you in motion? Every time you start and stop, start and stop and sometimes it's more like stop, stop, stop… It is harder to get the momentum back in your business. It's difficult to muster your creativity. It can be a nightmare to get the people on your team back in position, ready to work. If you can stay in motion no matter how slow or bad things get, you're going to find out that your compounding results will be so much greater than if you were doing numerous tasks at one time. Just think about it, a penny doubled is worth more than five million dollars. Your efforts, a little bit a day, are greater than you having one big push and stopping midstream. Compounded effort is literally the secret weapon of champions. Einstein said, compound interest is the 8th wonder of the world. I believe that compounding efforts is the secret weapon for making you a superhero in business. You have to remember every time you start a task and stop, you're delaying your ability to succeed. You have to keep going, you have to be like the little blue engine that thought he could. He kept telling himself, I think I can, I think I can, and he did not give up. Because of your everyday effort and consistency your reward will be so massive. Soon you will become a profit producer. Duplication, scaling and compounding efforts are business strategies that are going to keep your business running long term. They're definitely going to be the financial pillars that increase your revenue and create generational wealth.

REVELATION 11

Technology is the Bridge to Wealth

And I tell you, ask, and it will be given to you; seek,
and you will find; knock, and it will be opened to you.

Luke 11:9, ESV

In this day and age, we cannot deny that we are dependent on technology. We use our Smartphones has an extension of our physical being. However, when it comes to small businesses, we tend to underutilize technology when attracting customers, fulfilling orders and other systems required to run a six and seven figure business.

Tech Phobia

I had a disease called tech phobia. It was severe! I was scared of the different tools. I was also leery of investing in multiple tools that I was unclear on how to use. Indeed, shying away from technology was one of the biggest mistakes that I ever made. I was still stuck to the pen and paper mentality for way too long. So I invested in the team, learning as much as I could. Throughout the book you've heard the resounding fact that there's only so much that you can do on your own. There's only so many hours in a day that is awarded to you and you have a finite amount of energy. Tech tools will help you leverage those limitations. I found myself in the first years of business truly overwhelmed by all of the small tasks, tracking expenses, making graphics, communicating with groups of people, etc. It was so bad that I was even using written time sheets and spending hours calculating time for my employees. Today, it takes me about 15 minutes to do the same task. Finally, I realized that technology was the key to save time and an inexpensive way for me to overcome some of those obstacles I was having.

Changing Times

The times are changing! Think about what Redbox did to Blockbuster Video. When Redbox came on the scene Blockbuster Video stores closed everywhere around the world. Never did the media giant expect a little red kiosk to change the way we see movies. When you wanted to rent a movie, you had to get dressed, get in your car and drive to Blockbuster. Once you arrived you walked around the store until you made a selection. It could take hours. Using your membership, you would check it out and you could rent the movie for two days and bring it back. Then Redbox came on the scene and they had kiosk everywhere. No membership was needed. They were open twenty-four hours and all you need was a credit card. You can browse through their selection, pick a movie of your choice and take it home. No hassle! But times have changed yet again. I believe that Redbox is on the brink of extinction. With companies like Netflix and Hulu you can watch anything from anywhere. You can literally pick up any electronic device, in your pajamas, watch any movie or any T.V. show that you want for free or a minimum fee, with the click of a finger. Music is also readily available for your listening pleasure. You can even listen to CD's that have not been released in stores if you have some streaming services. We see this phenomenon in more than one industry. Think about how we exchange money. PayPal, Cash APP and other services have revolutionized the banking industry. You can create invoices, integrate payment tools on your website, collect and send funds with your phone or laptop. This Revelation includes a list of tools and websites that will help you on your way as you pursue your entrepreneurial journey. These tools are designed to give you the most bang for your buck when it comes to leveraging your time and being efficient. Look at this list and create your own to fill in gaps that will help your business grow.

There are tools for:

1. Customer Follow-up
2. Email List
3. Website Design
4. Graphic Design
5. Data Storage
6. Outsourcing Hubs
7. Project Management
8. Surveys
9. Completing Digital Forms
10. Sales and Online Shopping Carts
11. Payments
12. Bookkeeping
13. Payroll
14. Podcast Creation
15. Video Editing
16. Funnels Creation
17. Advertisements
18. Online Courses
19. Video Conferencing
20. AND SO MUCH MORE!

Consider how your business runs and what's working in your industry. Every industry is absolutely different and there are different tools that work better based on industry preference. Website platforms are important to consider. Certain websites will allow shopping carts, form completion, load videos and more. Make sure you choose the digitals tools that will best assist you in accomplishing your business goals. Choose a platform that will encompass each task.

Social Media

Social Media has changed the way we communicate and connect. It has become a major digital platform for people to know more about you and your services. You have to use social media in a way that it lets people know about you and your businesses. Social media lets your potential customer know more about what you do and what problem you can solve for them. People really don't care how much you know. They do care if what you know is what's going to ultimately help them fix their problem. Social Media is a free billboard. Use it to brand yourself and advertise your business.

Top Tips for using Social Media:

1. Determine how you want to use Social Media

2. Get to know your audience and what they need

3. Let people get to know you

4. Post consistently to engage followers

5. Create content that attracts and educates your follower

6. Use a content calendar for scheduling post

7. Engage in one-on-one follow-ups

8. Increase awareness of your brand, skills, products and services

9. Drive traffic to your website

10. Build your email list

11. Generate leads

12. Offer a product or services often

13. Build online communities

14. Use live streaming

15. Use exciting and relevant graphics

16. Use ads to widen your reach

Remember, technology is not your enemy, there's nothing to be afraid of. It is going to be the tool that allows you to reach nations, surpassing your community. You can reach the world for pennies compared to the cost for print advertising, billboards, radio, and television ads. Tech tools are going to allow you to cross into different geographic communities, economic classes, ethnic groups, and across industries. It is one way to break down those barriers. It will help you save money, make money, streamline tasks and increase scalability in your business. Technology is truly the bridge to wealth. There are thousands of online tools for business owners that increase productivity and decrease time and money spent. Tech tools can have you looking like a pro in no time. I have added tools over time to match the needs of my business. I will caution you to slowly integrate only what you need, or you will fall into a technology web of horrors. Check out each tool and see what fits your needs.

1. **Canva– https://www.canva.com**

Canva makes design simple for everyone. Create designs for web or print: blog graphics, presentations, Facebook covers, flyers, posters, invitations and so much more.

2. **WordPress– https://WordPress.com/com-vs-org**

WordPress powers more than 28% of the web, a figure that rises every day. Everything from simple websites, to blogs, to complex portals and enterprise websites, and even applications, are built with WordPress.

3. **Zoom– https://zoom.us**

Zoom unifies cloud video conferencing, simple online meetings, and cross platform group chat into one easy-to-use platform. They have several features including recording, share screen andmultiple presenters. My absolute favorite feature is their live stream integration with Facebook.

4. **Buffer– https://buffer.com**

Buffer makes it super easy to share on your social media pages. Keep your Buffer topped with social media post. You can pre-schedule a post so they will be uploaded throughout the day.

5. Calendly- https://calendly.com/ (Free Version Available)

Calendly is a scheduling software that enables its users to streamline their appointment schedules. Customers can schedule event types based on your customized availability schedule. Integrates with Google Calendar, Apps and websites easily.

6. MailChimp- https://mailchimp.com/ (Free Version Available)

MailChimp provides marketing automation for e-commerce businesses. Send beautiful emails, connect your e-commerce store, advertise, and build your brand. MailChimp makes it easy to create campaigns that connect with your audience at the right time and the right place. They are most known for email marketing and their automation capabilities. They integrate well with other apps to make sure all your lead generation ends up on your email list.

7. Google Drive- (Free-Connected to your Gmail account)

Google Drive is a personal cloud storage service from Google that lets users store and synchronize digital content across computers, laptops and mobile devices, including Android-powered tablet and smartphone devices.

8. Google Docs- (Free- Connected to your Gmail account)

Google Docs is a free Web-based application in which documents and spreadsheets can be created, edited and stored online. Files can be accessed from any computer with an Internet connection and a full-featured Web browser. Google Docs is compatible with most presentation software and word processor applications. There are Google Sheets, Presentation, Forms, Voice and much more!

9. Webinar Ninja- https://webinarninja.com

Webinar Ninja is the most advanced and complete webinar solution. Run live and evergreen webinars in minutes. Awesome list building tool with email opt-in. You can integrate pre-recorded videos or record live.

10. PayPal- www. PayPal.com

PayPal makes it easy to send and receive funds for goods and services. It has an invoicing feature and even has the ability to create custom online buttons and links that can be used to solicit payment, donation, registration, etc.

I highly recommend you have more than one way to accept payments. You never know if you will need another option. You don't ever want to be in a position where you cannot accept payments easily. Some platforms require you be verified. There is Stripe, CashApp, Square and many other options. PayPal will also offer business loans based on your business volume.

11. Quick Books Online- https://quickbooks.intuit.com/online (Free Trial)

QuickBooks is an accounting software geared mainly toward small and medium-sized businesses. It easily also calculates profit loss at a glance, monthly, quarterly and yearly.

12. ClickFunnels- http://bit.ly/phuclickfunnels (Free Trial)

ClickFunnels is the new generation of online tools. With the click of a button, you can instantly create dozens of different types of sales funnels, including opt-in funnels, sales funnels, webinar funnels, membership sites, and more! This all-inclusive tool has saved me thousands of dollars by combining several paid services.

13. SocialSteeze- https://www.socialsteeze.net

SocialSteeze has a great solution for anyone looking to grow their Instagram account. Whether you're an influencer, a brand, or any other individual looking for more followers and better engagement, they have you covered - regardless of your industry, your brand, or your goals. They don't sell fake followers. SocialSteeze has spent time developing specialized marketing techniques to help you see real, targeted, engaged results.

14. FormSite- https://www.FormSite.com

Create your form to fit any style. Try for free, no download required. Easy web forms & surveys. 100+ pre-built templates. All forms are responsive. Easy drag & drop editor. Great for surveys, too. Download & share data. Types: HTML Forms, Web Forms, Registration Forms, Survey Forms. You will be able to share a secure link to your form or embed it into a page on your site. Your forms are automatically responsive for all device types: desktops, tablets, and phones. We handle hosting your form and processing your results.

15. Bitly- https://bitly.com/

This tool has saved me so much time and money. No more buying domain names for each event or project. Bitly links help businesses brand, measure, and optimize their links to build the best possible customer experience.

16. Fiverr -https://www.Fiverr.com/

Fiverr is the world's largest freelance services marketplace for lean entrepreneurs to focus on growth and create a successful business at affordable costs. There are hundreds of services from graphic design, voice over, editing, data entry. You can read reviews and see samples of each freelancers work and even ask questions prior to committing to a project.

17. Upwork- https://www.upwork.com/

Upwork allows business owners to hire freelancers for anything and everything. Whether you need web development, graphics designers, social media managers, etc., there is probably someone on Upwork who can help growth hack your company. Their review, bidding and reference system allows you to have the ease of mind in vetting anyone you choose to work with.

With freelancers all over the world you get business task done around the clock. You can hire for short-term projects, full time work or create an entire team.

18. Trello- https://trello.com/

Trello provides team and task management platforms. Trello can create various boards and cards, set due dates, add notes, etc. Trello allows structuring and keeping track of tasks to be as simple as possible. This tool gives you the ability to see the progress of a project in totality and/or by individual contribution.

19. Kickstarter- https://www.kickstarter.com/

Kickstarter is a funding platform for creative projects. Everything from films, books, games, and music to art, design, and technology. Kickstarter is full of ambitious, innovative, and imaginative ideas that are brought to life through the direct support of others. Everything on Kickstarter must be a project with a clear goal, like making an album, a book, or a work of art. Funding on Kickstarter is an all-or-nothing funding campaign. No one will be charged for a pledge towards a project unless it reaches its funding goal. This way, creators always have the budget they scoped out before moving forward.

20. DocuSign- https://www.docusign.com

There is no reason to travel around the world to get a signature with tools like DocuSign. Simply upload a Microsoft Word, PDF, or other common document format from your computer or from popular file- sharing sites like Box, Dropbox, Google

Drive, and OneDrive. You can add in signatures, initials or other information retrieval spaces. Send to your recipient and have them sign. This tool is great for contracts and so much more.

REVELATION 12

The Profit Producers Blueprint

Write the vision, and make it plain upon
tablets, that he may run that readeth it.
Habakkuk 2:2, ASV.

There is a blueprint for being a profit producer. A blue-print is a technical drawing, an architectural plan or an engineering design to build a structure. When I think about blueprints, they are often difficult to decipher to the un-trained eye because there are so many complex elements. If you not an architect, you might wonder, what does it all mean? A blueprint is so intricately laid out by its visionaries that it's more technical and detailed than any paragraph or set of words could be. It speaks to the designer in a way text could not. This is how you have to be about your business; precise and planned to the smallest detail. Business is multifaceted. You need to plan out several aspects of your business to make sure you have a solid structured design to produce a profit. These are the key elements that every entrepreneur should consider when they are growing their business, even from the start-up or expansion phase.

Vision

Your vision is the most important and foundational principle when creating a business. Habakkuk 2:2, ASV, clearly instructs, "Write the vision, and make it plain upon tablets, that he may run that readeth it." This process may take some time but everything else hinges on your vision. Have a clear concise understanding of what your business is, who you're serving and why you're serving these people. Being crystal clear will help you construct your core message, branding, products and services. It will also help you to know what opportunities are just right for you in your business. We talked about it in Revelation 8, in *Connecting Cultivating and Cash Out*. It is extremely important to target your ideal customer in your ideal market, but with a clear vision and with your "why" clearly defined. Ask yourself the following questions:

1. Why are you starting this business?

2. What do you hope to gain?

3. What problems are solving?

4. What's influencing you to make this journey?

5. Are you making decisions from a pure place?

6. What is the end goal?

7. Who or what do you need to run this business successfully?

Once you know the answers to these questions, you are in a better position to be a profit producer. The profit will not come as long as you are confused. Confusion repels money. When you don't have a clear vision, you will waste a lot of time, energy and money doing the WRONG things and getting the WRONG results. However, if you focus on the vision, you will be catapulted into a continuous stream of wealth.

Operational Plan

Once your vision is created, you have to have a plan. Most people construct a business plan for their endeavors. But an operational plan is much more. It comprises all the elements of your business plan, but also includes how and who will execute it. I don't just mean an Itsy-Bitsy Teeny-Weeny "this is what I want to do plan." This plan must include every facet of your business including growth and an exit strategies. Profit Producers don't close businesses, we sell them. You don't want to start a business thinking like, "I'm a mom-and-pop shop. I'm only going to serve a few customers." Even if you start small, plan to end as a giant in your industry. Consider these five questions:

1. What sets you apart from competitors?

2. How will you stand out in the crowd?

3. What will be your money magnet? (Products and Services)

4. What systems will you use to serve and reach the masses?

5. Who will support you in growing your business?

Profit Plan

Revenue and profits are not the same. Profits are what you have left when the bills are paid and the dust settles. You need to establish a budget for your business. Your budget should include fixed costs, payroll, facilities, raw cost of goods and services and other operational expenses. It is also wise to invest 3 to 5 percent of your income if self-development. This could be in the form of mentor, conferences, classes or books. You must identify cycles and seasons in your business. Realize when business is slow and when business is thriving. This will help you establish a great financial plan for your business. You need to know how much capital you need to raise to start your business, your anticipated monthly or quarterly operation costs, how much revenue you are projecting to generate. How can you fail proof this plan? You have to layer your operational plan to compensate for the unexpected. Sometimes we have a profit plan for our business that doesn't work, so you need to have some alternate routes or opportunities. What other products, services or skills do you have that you can monetize while you're getting your business up and running? It may be also time to expand or revolutionize your business model. Remember what happened to Blockbuster when they tried to hold on to an antiquated and outdated business model. We have to evolve with the needs and desires of our customers.

Accountability

Journal the Journey

You have to do the work when it comes to generating revenue. Nike says, "Just Do It!" I love that mantra. Indirectly, it says, don't worry about the excuses, don't worry about if it's raining outside, there is no need to worry about the competition. Just do your best. One of the ways that you can "Just Do It!" is document every day. Document what you're doing; your ideas, processes, success and failures. You cannot avoid your future failures unless you go back and look at that documentation and course-correct. More importantly, you cannot duplicate your success without documentation of what you've done.

One of the most powerful things I did when my life was upside down was to the journal. I begin to write my way out of situations and formulate a formula for success. I admonish you to journal, not just personally, but professionally. Professionally you should track your journey. How many customers did you have today? How many sales? Who did you talk to? Where did you post? Create a written or electronic document that allows you to journal the aspects of your business. Personally, record the emotional and spiritual journey. These moments will become the same testimonies that draw people to you. Just think less than 10 years ago I was homeless with $12 dollars to my name. I was broken into a million pieces and cried a billion tears, I persevered, I know you can too.

Personal Accountability

Personal Accountability is key to create the discipline needed to reach your goals. Have a scorecard for your plan. Every time you schedule a task need to score yourself. You can score yourself daily or weekly. List everything you need to do and at the end of the day or week calculate your completion score. If you have ten things and you only did seven, your proficiency rate is 70%. In a week you could have hundreds of tasks to complete. In order to really be effective in business, you need to accomplish your tasks at about an 85% rate. It goes back to that compounding effort. When you plan, make the correct choices and exhibit the correct behaviors, success will come. Consistent repeat the right strategies and over time, you will see the results that you want. As you do the work, score your proficiency. Don't forget to delegate to elevate. Use your team to get more done. I guarantee the scorecard strategy will increase your effectiveness and efficiency. Your business will reward you with revenues and riches.

The Importance of a Mentor or Coach

Accountability is a major factor that divides the successful from the "not yet" successful. Think back to the blueprint for a building. Once an architect makes a plan, they have to be certified and stamped by an engineer. It's very important that we have our plans certified and stamped not just by an engineer in the physical, but by God's engineering. Make sure you take those plans before the Lord and have Him look over them and have Him help you every step of the way when you are constructing those plans. I love the fact that God has given us a free will, and He's given us the ability to choose His plan for our lives. He's made us very wise and creative just like Him. He's given us the ability to come to Him and ask Him questions and to make sure that our plan is spiritually validated. As you work through your plan as a profit producer, make sure that you have a clear vision over both the thought-out plan, and its layered alternatives. Having a mentor or coach is more valuable than I can explain. I have hired spiritual, fitness and business coaches. Each time, they were able to walk me through my uncharted territory because of their wisdom and experience. According to the Institute of Coaching, 80% of people who receive coaching report increased self-confidence. 70% benefit from improved work performance, relationships, and more effective communication skills. 86% recouped their investment on coaching in their business. Coaches and Mentors help see from a different perspective helping you navigate through the rocky moments. I can remember how I struggled for seven years to open *Imagine Me Academy*. Year after year, I experienced the shame, frustration and time loss of not birthing my dream. I began to get so upset when people asked, "When are you going open?" It was like a slap in my face. Each time, I felt a sense of failure. It was the mentors in my life that got me on track every time. They helped me strategize you to climb out of the rut and start again. They held me accountable to the vision and to why I wanted to start the business in the first place. Fast forward to today, the same business I wanted to give up on has created massive income and allowed me to live the life I desire. Never underestimate the power of help. Look at the areas of your life and business you need the most help. This is the area you need to increase accountability and mentor relationships.

Conclusion

Every step on your entrepreneurial journey is an adventure and some parts of the adventure will be scary. Other experience will be exhilarating. Each step will definitely be an adventure, nonetheless. You'll experience some failures on this journey. You will learn many lessons and have growth and success. Every day you will have to decide whether to pursue or to retreat. I remember a story where God had to tell David to pursue his enemies. David and his army had lost everything. Tragically, even women and the children have been stolen. His one questions to God was "What should I do?" God's command was to pursue and go and get everything that the enemy stole from him.

Pursue! That's why I'm encouraging you to do. Go and pursue your dreams. Take what that you want from life, it's yours for the taking. God has already given you the power and the permission to create the life that you want.

This pursuit cannot be half-hearted. It cannot be undercalculated. It will take all of your mind, your body and spirit. The spirit is willing, but the flesh is weak. Some days you going to have to drag yourself out of bed and make yourself do the work. You won't feel like making the calls answering emails and updating your website, but you have to. Get up, dust yourself off and do what it takes to pursue your dreams.

Achieving your goals will be 80 percent mindset and 20 percent activity. Once you can conquer your mind, you will inevitably achieve everything that you want. Completing this book is the beginning of a new beginning. This book is twelve revelations by *The Millionaire Midwife,* it's a clear view into some of the successes and the failures I've had. It's the most tender part of me for the world to see. It's also a way to positively impact your success and longevity in business and any businesses you may pursue in the future.

Nine out of every ten businesses will fail. Trust me, I've had my share of failures before the businesses were successful. In every failure, I learned a lesson and forged relationships. I also had the revelations revealed in this book and developed a solid resolve. I was destined to succeed. I saw people succeed and I asked myself, "why not me?" There was nothing at all separating me from my dream… but me and my will to win. There is nothing separating you either.

The revelations I share will help you shift your mindset and employ strategies that will assist you in effectively executing your plan both professionally and personally. It will dramatically increase your results and continue to increase your profit margin for years and years to come.

As *The Millionaire Midwife*, I desire to see you become a profit producer. Yes, that's what I call my mentees, the profit producers. A profit producer is a capable of creating wealth throughout their business. A profit producer creates a business that allows them to enjoy the richness of life as well as the prosperity of money. So, you never settle for anything less than what you're capable of.

It is my sincere desire and goal that through these ten revelations that you will be able to create the life that you desire from your business. It is my earnest prayer that this book will help you transition from where you are to where you want to be in life.

Stop waiting, the time is now! Remember, the shift in your thinking will change the shift in your actions. It is that course of action that will bring you from where you are directly into your destiny and make you your own profit producer. As a midwife, I have to tell you, birthing this level of success may be painful, it may be easy or difficult to carry. You may experience some birthing pains along the way, and you even may have some contractions that will make you want to stop and give up. You cannot abort or miscarry the mission. There is a greatness within you only you can birth into the world. I am here to encourage you and help you push into greatness. I wholly accept the calling as *The Millionaire Midwife* to help you become the profit producer, I know that you desire to be.

About the Author

BRANDY WOODS-SMITH is a charismatic and passionate educator, entrepreneur, speaker and consultant. She is known as a thought leader, change agent, community developer and the *Millionaire Midwife*.

Her career as an educator began long before she received her first class in 2000. Her passion for learning was ignited when she was in high school and worked with the Future Teachers of Texas. Her first students were teachers. She toured Texas speaking to educators as the 1995 -1996 Miss Future Teacher of Texas.

Ms. Woods attended Jarvis Christian College in East Texas. She double majored in Education and Mathematics. After graduation, she was selected to start on graduate work at TEXAS A & M through their teacher induction program. She finished her Master in Education Administration in 2005 through the University of Phoenix and completed her administrative certification program through Region IV. She taught a total of 9 years (2nd-8th grade) and has served as the Secondary Math Specialist for 3 years. In 2011 she was hired as the Director of Curriculum and Instruction and was later promoted to Director of School Operations.

After serving in public education for 13 years, Woods opened Imagine Me Academy in 2013 and her second location in 2014. Imagine Me Academy is a premiere private educational organization, providing services start at Early Child Hood through Middle School, a homeschool co-op and services for special needs children. Imagine Academy partners with DECA, HeadStart, Crosby ISD, Dallas ISD, Houston ISD, Fort Bend ISD, Barrett Civic Lead, Woodforest National Bank and other organization to support community develop on a local, state and National level.

In her quest to help other aspiring entrepreneur achieve success and profitability, she founded Powerhouses United. Powerhouses United is a business incubator design to gives education, resources, connection and funding opportunities for small business. Powerhouses United is committed to teach financial literacy, giving each family an opportunity for financial stability and wealth accumulation.

With her wide range of experience public education, public speaking and training over that last 20 years, Woods was sought after as an educational and business consultant. She currently consults with school districts, private schools, curriculum companies, and small business through Imagine Me Academy, Powerhouses

United and Project Imagine Me 501 (c) (3). Her consulting is designed to help other companies achieve their business goals through education, resources, strategic planning and execution.

Believe BIG! Expect BIG! Do BIG! is the mantra she lives by. Woods says, "Although BIG is not the most eloquent word, it gets the vision across clearly! With belief in my heart, the work of my hands, and the words in my mouth. I will accomplish what I am commissioned to do: Motivate! Educate! Produce!"

Work with the Millionaire Midwife:

- Private Coaching
- Group Coaching
- Daycare Consulting
- Speaking Engagements
- Conference Host
- Media Guest

www.PowerhousesUnited.com

powerhousesunited@gmail.com

Stay connected by joining *The Make Money Moves* **community!**

Linktr.ee/brandywoods.1908

www.ingramcontent.com/pod-product-compliance
Lightning Source LLC
Chambersburg PA
CBHW031945190326
41519CB00007B/668